Stories From the Living Room

A GOLDEN HERITAGE FROM THE OLD WEST

Second Edition

STORIES OF PIONEERS, HOMESTEADERS,

AND COWBOYS—REAL STORIES OF REAL PEOPLE

A Narrative History of the Old West

By
JON GARATE

Library of Congress Control Number: 2006907126
ISBN: Hardcover   978-1-4257-2816-8
               Softcover   978-1-4257-2815-1

To order additional copies of this book, contact:
Xlibris Corporation
1-888-795-4274
www.Xlibris.com
Orders@Xlibris.com
33797

CONTENTS

CREDITS

This work is dedicated to my kids, Shawn, Jonny, Trini, Tony, Tonya, and Maryann—and to all my grandkids, present and future.

Credit goes to Mom and Dad for being homesteaders and pioneers, and being the best example of those values and principles, eternal and good, which were exemplified by the founders and builders of the American West.

Credit goes to all the other pioneers and homesteaders of the Madeline Plains who lived and told their stories.

A great big Thank You to my wife Connie for proof-reading all my work, and letting me know when I had things written in totally incomprehensible American (English).

Thanks also to grand-daughters Alexis and Danae for helping with proofreading.

A thank you also to the Almighty, and to America—for this great country that provided such a rich and beautiful legacy.

CLAIMERS AND DISCLAIMERS

This book is intended for reading by audiences of all ages. Originally, it was mainly for my own kids, but now I make it available for the general public, and I also make it available to schools, since I put on living history programs of stories and songs of the cowboys and the Old West in local schools for the fourth graders, who are at that grade level, studying California history.

Therefore, I have the dilemma of trying to maintain a "G" rating, and still tell it like it really was, and make it meaningful to adults also.

I have included what might be considered by "modern civilized" folk some grossly graphic descriptions in the book, although they would not be considered such by adults or children of the pioneer era. They are just a part of everyday life as it was. Since I grew up and lived among the pioneers, it is not entirely possible for me to know what might be gross to people today, so I've had my wife help me do the screening. For the most part, we believe the book to be G rated.

Note to Teachers and parents:

I have tried to identify such gross descriptions so that you can screen the book before presenting it to your students or children and blot out those things if you like.

We didn't take many pictures that I could share with you, so I have tried to enhance some stories by pen and ink drawings. I consider myself to be a lousy artist, and so any resemblance to real people or events would be purely accidental.

As an old time cowboys from the Madeline Plains, I am exempt from being politically correct. I have an official permit to be un-pc, and make no apologies for not using "he or she" all the time. It takes too long, and wastes paper. And besides, pioneer women wouldn't be offended by un-pc, and I hope you ain't either. Further, my Indian friends ain't offended at being called Indians. After all, when using the pc term, "Native American", the word *American* is as un-Indian as the term *Indian* itself. My friends are Maidus, Paiutes, Modocs, Kickapoos, Klamaths, and so on. They for sure ain't Native *Americans*!

INTRODUCTION

Note: Before reading any further here at the beginning, you might like to turn to the back of the book, and read the Glossary. It will give you a little taste of the flavor of this work, and give you a little understanding of some of the cowboy and pioneer lingo included in the following pages.

There, now that you've got that done, let's turn to a serious note for a few minutes, and give you a little background of what this book is and how it came to be. Or if you want to skip the serious stuff, just go right on to the Preface, and chapter one.

The Madeline Plains are located in the northeastern area of California. It is a very remote high desert area, about 150 miles north of Reno Nevada, just inside the California line. It is a tough country—a mean climate country—hot and dry in the summer and cold—very cold in the winter time. The elevation of the Plains, or Flat as they are called by the locals is 5200 feet, and then the mountains of the Warner range rise up surrounding the kidney shaped salt desert Flat. It is not impressive in size like the Great Plains. North to south the Plains measure about 20 miles, and probably about the same east to west.

The Plains were at best marginal for agricultural use. The land and climate was so harsh that even the Indians didn't want it. There never was any quarrel with the Indians over the white man settling in this area. Nevertheless, man has an unquenchable desire to own land, and this was one of the last areas to be offered in by way of the homestead act. Both my grandfather and father were homesteaders.

Because of it's remote location, the Plains remained pretty much isolated from *civilization* until past midway of the 20th century. It was cattle and sheep country. Ranches were few and far between. The people were pioneers, homesteaders, cowboys and sheepmen of the traditional American West—fiercely independent and self reliant. Even in my day, and I wasn't born until 1945, most of the farms and ranches hadn't mechanized. All the work was still done by hand, or with horses. Electric service didn't arrive at the south end of the Plains until around 1960, and real telephone service much later than that.

Imagine a community if you will, where there are no policemen, lawyers, judges, or jails. There were no streetlights, paved roads, and few automobiles upon the roads. Except for the postal service, the road maintenance service, and the Bureau of Land Management, there were no government services, and the BLM was more often considered the enemy, instead of a friend.

There were no doctors, insurance companies, or churches. There were, however three towns, and each had a bar. There wasn't a house on the Plains with doors that locked. There was however, at least one gun in every home, and people, even including the kids understood the proper use it. In spite of all this lack of structure and government regulation, nobody ever shot nobody, and people managed to get along with each other a lot better than folks down in the flatlands where they had all kinds of laws, government services, police, lawyers, and jails and such. The flatlanders considered themselves to be *civilized* and they in fact labeled us hicks, hillbillies, and wild cowboys.

You could say we were a lawless bunch, but in reality we were simply beyond the law. We lived by our own rules, which were few and unwritten, and mostly even unspoken. The Golden Rule, even though we never heard of it, was practiced and lived better than most *civilized* folks who go to church every week. That is not to say that people didn't have disagreements—sure they did. And they had their own ways of settling disputes, which at the extreme, would involve a couple of guys boxin' one another's ears a bit. This might sound barbaric to you modern people, but I can tell you this—it was considered cowardly to even think about using a gun or a weapon other than what you were born with to solve such problems. It was a lot safer on the Plains than it is in our schools and other *civilized* places of today. The fact is, that on the Plains it was considered ok to dislike a neighbor, but never to the point that you wouldn't help out if he was in trouble.

People were very independent, but in cases of any personal disaster, the whole community would turn out to help. Work was highly respected, and idleness was shunned like the plague. There was a saying, "If you don't work, you don't eat". And no matter what your physical abilities, or your mental capacities, even the most unfit or misfit rambler could find some kind of work on the ranches, and a vacant bunkhouse or old cabin to live in. That was our "welfare" system, which had no place for shirkers or idlers.

Life was hard on the Plains, but it was good. It had almost nothing to do with money or things, both of which were very scarce. There are some things I would never want to go back to—like not having refrigerators, and many other marvels of modern technology. What I would go back to in a short sweet minute if I could, is the way that people were, and the ways they treated each other.

There was this sort of game that went on between us and the more refined folks who lived way off in *civilization*. It was more of a contest of opinions about which way of life was best—our primitive backward ways, or the industrialized technological ways of our citified relatives and acquaintances. The debate, if you will, dates back into pre-history, and lived until the world was pretty much industrialized. Now I fear most people will never get to participate in this marvelous game.

We were often called names, like ignorant farmers, hicks, hillbillies, wild cowboys, etc. And we came up with our own names in return, like dudes, flatlanders, city slickers and so on. Usually it was in fun, or semi-fun, but occasionally got fairly serious. Sadly to say, there are so few old time cowboys, homesteaders, and pioneers left, that you civilized city slickers have forgotten how to do the debate, and I miss it. You have won. But I still don't think it is because your ways are better. We just couldn't compete with industrialization. So if you occasionally feel me shooting little barbs at civilization, technology, the government, bureaucracies, and citified ways in general, please don't take it personal. Just have some fun with it. Revive the age old debate and see if you can truly defend your way of life. Remember, you don't have to worry about losing since you've already won. But beware! We then, and I now, aren't as ignorant as we were accused of being. And there really and truly are some things out of the old ways that are worth bringing back. As I said before, most especially, the way people treated each other.

So now having presented this very condensed background, I'd like to now tell you how this book of stories came about. I got to realizing a few years back how my kids, who were raised in the age of television, even though they all had been to the old homestead ranch, would never be able to fully experience an *evening in the living room*, as we used to. By the time my kids came along, electricity and other elements of *civilization* had arrived on the Plains, and people had changed, sadly to say, forever. So I began putting in print things about a way of life which is now history. This work has finally evolved into this, the second edition of Stories From The Living Room. I wish it were possible for each of you who read this book, to spend an evening with me and friends in my living room, making old time home-made country music, and telling the stories of life. Since that isn't possible, would you please turn off the TV now and then, invite some friends over and have a good meal, a good visit, and tell some stories from your own lives.

In the meantime, happy reading.

PREFACE

This book is not a history. It is not a biography. Maybe it could be called a narrative history. In reality it is a book of stories—oral histories. In the days before civilization infected the old ways with such things as television, the art of telling stories from life's experiences was a prominent form of entertainment. Oh, we didn't call it storytelling. We just called it visiting. Neighbors lived miles apart. It was a real treat to invite a neighboring family over for supper, and then after supper, gather in the living room to visit. We talked about the weather, and politics—the two things which heavily affected our lives—and the two things about which we could do almost nothing. The saying was that some "bureaucrat" could sign some order with less than an ounce of ink, and ruin our lives.

Invariably after some time of discussing the weather and politics, the conversation would turn to reminiscing. Someone would tell a story, which would bring to mind some other incident, and another, and another. There was no particular pattern. Some little thing in one story would bring a memory to someone else, and then off that person would go with a story of his own. The stories thus might seem to be random. This could go on for hours. People knew how to laugh at their follies. My father was in my eyes the greatest of all the old timers for telling a story. I learned the art from him. I hope that I have learned to do as he did—that is to find humor in all of life's experiences—both the good ones and the bad ones.

It is my hope that I can create for you the reader, at least some of that atmosphere that existed in the living room, and that I might inspire someone to pick up the tradition of telling stories from life. It is my belief that anyone who has lived past the age of eight, has had unique and marvelous experiences in life that make for stories worth telling. I hope you begin to recognize the wonder of your life's experiences. I'm sure you have them. I hope that you can see how it is possible to have a real miserable experience, and then look back on it and find the humor that is there. You might have to look pretty hard at some experiences, but it is worth it. It is there, I promise you.

Many of the included stories come from the era of pioneers and homesteaders, cowboys, and Indians. All the stories are true, based on the memory of the person who told them, myself included. The stories that happened before my time, I am retelling as I remember hearing them as they were told originally by the old timers before me.

So come on into the living room, sit back, get comfy and let's have a real good time.

1

A TOUGH OLD COWBOY *CAN* APOLOGIZE

I want to start out with this particular story as a tribute to Dad, (1906-1988) the greatest storyteller of all. Although this story was always told by my mother, Dad always had a particular little fillyossify that he would add in at the end of the story.

One day, many years ago, Dad was getting ready to move a bunch of cows down the lane that runs by the house. He asked Mom to stand in an open gate to keep the cows from going into the field next to the house as he drove them by. The problem arose that there were two gates open on that particular day, one into the lower field, and the one into the upper field. Mom went to the first gate which she saw open which happened to be the one into the upper field. Dad came driving the cows down the lane, and of course cows will always do what you don't want them to, and naturally saw the opportunity in the open gate to the lower field, and away they went. Dad, seeing what was happening, came galloping after them, yelling a few unkind words to Mom as he charged by, about "Why the #*" can't you get in the gate like I asked you". Now as fate would have it there happened to be about an inch of snow on the ground that day and in the mad rush to round up the cows, Dad's horse slipped on the snow, fell on Dad, breaking his leg, and leaving him lying in the snow. Now, Mom, not one to miss a choice opportunity walked out into the field to where Dad was, and assessing that he had a broken leg, but nothing more, she says to him, "Have you got something you'd like to say to me."?

I have to tell you here that the old time ranchers were an independent, hardheaded, strong-minded bunch, not known for making apologies or speaking gentle words of kindness. It was a tough world, and the people were tough—on the outside. On the inside, people were much more kindly, honest, and generous than most *civilized* folks, but only people with the tough pioneer spirit survived on the harsh, high desert Madeline Plains.

Anyhow, on *that* day *Dad apologized*! Said he figured Mom was going to leave him there to freeze in the snow if he didn't—and since he did actually apologize she didn't let him die. She put him on a sled and dragged him to the house, and eventually got him to a doctor to get his leg fixed.

At the end of Mom telling that story, Dad always got a little teasing from whoever was there, and that's when he would say "The secret to life

1

is being able to look back and find the humor in a situation that wasn't funny at all, at the time it happened, and *that* situation wasn't funny. I had to apologize or she was going to let me freeze to death". And he'd laugh right along with everybody else.

2

A MAN'S WORLD—MAYBE, MAYBE NOT

RUNNING WATER

The day came when people began to pipe water from the windmill into an elevated tank, and then from the tank into the house. That was called running water. I don't know what the other kind of water was called. Walking water? Or sleeping water? Or idle water?

In those days, my best friend was Larry Morgan. We spent a lot of time at each others homes when we were growing up—I think you'd call it a sleepover. His mom, Dorothy made the best pancakes on the Plains.

When people began to get the *running water* I remember more than once, Dorothy saying to her husband, "Tom, when are we gonna get *running water* in *our* house"?

Tom's answer was always the same. "You got *running water*! You see that bucket there behind the stove. You grab that bucket and run right down to the well, fill 'er up, and run right back up here with it." And that's just what she did—raised 4 kids with her kind of *running water*. She never seriously complained. Tom, being the great mechanic that he was, could have easily piped water into the house. He wouldn't do it though—didn't want his wife gettin' all spoiled by modern gadgets.

Oh, I know!! Right now you are saying "How sexist—how chauvinistic!" But it wasn't so. It may have seemed like a mans world by some definitions, but the women were much more liberated then, than women of today. They could—and did do—any of the work that a man did, and got the same pay—next to nothing. Beyond that, they could be a wife and a mother. There was tremendous respect given to motherhood, and wifedom in that world. If you want to know more about how it worked you'll have to get my book, *Filly-ossifies of an Old Time Cowboy* when I get it published.

FLAT BISCUITS—MAYBE IT REALLY *WASN'T* A MAN'S WORLD

Gordon Locke was the Cow-boss on the Dodge Ranch. In my youth, I worked summers there as a hay-hand, but Gordon knew I was a pretty fair cowhand, so when he needed extra help he'd ask for me, and I'd spend a day or two in the saddle every now and then. I really liked working for him, because he was a really good cowboy, and it was a joy to watch him ride and rope. Gordon was a cowboy all the way, bowlegged, swagger, and talk all about horses, cows, ropin' and ridin'. Even when he sat down at the table for a meal, he'd come up beside his chair, and swing his right leg up and over the back of the chair to sit down in it—like as if he was mounting his horse.

Gordon's wife Rusty did the cooking, and like most ranch cooks, she was terrific. Plumb good eatin' is what it was. We had all sat down to dinner this one day, all in our places, and anxious to get at all that good grub. Gordon was at the head of the table, mounted into his chair as usual. We were gettin' right into the chowin' down, when old Gordon asked Rusty to hand him a biscuit. Now it so happened that there were two plates of biscuits on the table, one filled with flat baking powder biscuits, and the other with beautiful fluffy raised rolls. So Rusty, sittin' across the corner from Gordon, picked up a nice fluffy roll, and placed it on his plate. Well, Gordon was thinking of one of the other ones, and he picked up the roll and sailed it right onto Rusty's plate. "Not *that* one", He says. "I meant one of them *flat* ones". Rusty, got this kind of funny look on her face. Very deliberately she reached down, picked up that roll off her plate, set it on the table, made a fist, and—*wham, wham, wham*—she hammered that roll as flat as a silver dollar, picked it back up and, sailed it, kerplunk, right back onto Gordon's plate . . . . The rest of that meal was the quietest I ever sat through in all my years of ranching.

There was a certain line that a man ought not to cross and Gordon had crossed it. Nobody dared talk him about it. But everybody knew.

3

SOME OF THE MORE
ECCENTRIC CHARACTERS

SADDLE WORN OLD HORSE THIEF

You had to be a little crazy to think you could scratch a living out of the earth in that high desert country. Some people came and tried, got smart and left. Those that stayed became eccentric characters. Every last one of them—no exceptions.

One such was Sock Harris. Socrates was his given name, or so I was told. Seems like kind of a sophisticated name for a horse thief. Maybe that's why he ended up being known as Sock. Actually, he was a respectable horse trader—sometimes—sometimes not. He had a special attraction and devotion to horses, and if you stop and think about it, they really are magnificent creatures. I think he just couldn't resist assuming ownership of any horse he could get his hands on. I expect he always had some kind of excuse as to why he had possession of your horse.

Like the time he *borrowed* a couple of work horses from my Grandpa. The problem was that he simply kept *forgetting* to return them. Grandpa kept pestering him and finally, Sock being the *respectable* horse trader that he was finally showed up at our ranch with a team of work horses for Grandpa. A beautiful team of horses they were too—better than the ones he'd originally *borrowed*. Grandpa worried that Sock might have *borrowed* this team from somebody too, and anticipated that that particular somebody might happen by the ranch someday and accuse Grandpa of stealing them. Gladly, that never happened, so maybe old Sock came by them honestly. We never knew for sure.

When I first met Sock, I was just a kid, and he was an old man. By this time, his mind had sorta gone on vacation, and so he was living, albeit against his will, in the County Hospital in Susanville. That's where people went in those days when they had no family, and got too old to take care of themselves. We visited the hospital every time we went to town because of our family friend, Frank Amias who was also there.

Sock kind of took a liking to me and always had a horse story to tell. The gist of the story was always the same, finally coming around to old Sock having a bunch of horses out on some ranch and he needed to get outa there (the hospital) and take care of them real urgent like. And since *they* had taken away his horse and saddle, he needed my help. He'd say "You see that bunch of horses up there"? Pointing to the hill behind the hospital. "That white one's mine. I want you to go up there and bring him down here for me, and help me find my saddle. I gotta get out to the Dodge Ranch and take care of my horses".

Of course there weren't really any horses *up there*, but old Sock could see something, and it looked like horses to him. It was a wonderful game for a young boy and an old horse thief. "I can't see the white horse, where is he"? I'd say, and he'd come back "He's right there by that big juniper tree, see?" Pointing up the hill again, and then he'd describe the whole bunch of 'em to me. Finally, after hearing about all of his horses, and it was time to go, I'd tell him I'd bring his horse down as soon as I could. I wished there really was a white horse for him. We'd have surely rode off together on some great adventure.

That White Horse Is Mine

DAYS WORK CHAWIN' TOBACCER

Harv Howard was one of the cowboys that I had occasion to ride with. I was just a kid when I knew Harv too, but I was an ok cowhand myself, able to do a man's share of the work. Harv, like most of the cowboys, had a string of horses, and one time he let me ride one of his horses, a beautiful sorrel filly, full of life, and boy did she know how to work. You had to hold her back some because she was so eager. I secretly hoped that old Harv might take a liking to me and give me that horse, and worked really hard to try to impress him. I think he took a liking to me alright, but he liked the filly more. I could see why. She was a real jim-dandy.

Gross rated story—*maybe*. You'll hafta decide for yourself.

Old Harv had a full beard, and he chewed Days-O-Work chewing tobacco (*Days Work* is what you called it). It came in a compressed cake, called a plug, and old Harv would tear off a big chunk and stuff it in one cheek, and another chunk and stuff it in the other cheek—looking kinda like a chipmunk gathering nuts. Sometimes it was hard to understand him. He talked a little slobbery with all that chaw in his mouth. Every so often he'd *kerspit* a huge stream of tobacco juice for *forty feet*. Well, a long way for sure. His beard was white except for on his chin where brown tobacco juice dribbled down, and sometimes dripped off onto his shirt.

As far as I know, old Harv never married, though it was said that he spent a few days (and nights) in Reno once, where a somewhat clever *lady of the night* took him for all his money. (Do I hafta claim that as R rated if I say *lady of the n*ight?)

BILL ZIRKE

At the corner of the lane to the west of our house was an old wagon trail leading up and over the pass between Spanish Springs Peak, and Morgan Buttes. Just down out of the mountain on the other side is where Bill Zirke had his homestead. Bill never owned a car. He traveled in a buggie pulled by a pair of work horses. He smoked a pipe which had a very sweet smell. He was a bachelor, and a very good cook. Bill would always tell you how the weather was going to be, and what the latest news was. He "Hoid it ober der box". The *box* was the old battery powered radio that he had.

Bill, like all of us had a pretty clear idea of how mixed up the modern *civilized* world was in the flatlands below our secluded mountains. "People go out into der yard to eat, and come into der house to take a s___", (number two) He'd say. (Do I get to keep my G rating if I do it like that?)

For many generations, people had eaten meals in the house, and used the outhouse for doing those duties that belonged,—*not* in the house. One thing for sure, you never heard of an outhouse gettin' stopped up and flooding sewage through the house. And have you noticed to what ends people go to make the bathroom seem like something other than what it really is—a stinky outhouse moved *into* the house where it don't belong—very often right next to the kitchen, of all places. And wastin' all that water to carry the *stuff* off to a place where somebody else has to deal with it. *Civilization* is such an enigma. Mysterious too. And strange.

BIG JOHN

Big John worked for the railroad. He was a big man. He and his wife Loraine, and their niece, Eloise who lived with them, were black by race. Themselves, and my family being Basque, were sometimes the butt of ethnic jokes, but nobody ever did anything to hurt anybody as far as I know. Everybody was the butt of a joke at some time or other. We had some Arkies, and Okies, and some Tennessee hillbillies, and people from various European countries. Everybody got some teasing from time to time about how they talked, or where they had come from.

Big John could've snapped you in two like a toothpick if he wanted . . . but he didn't. He was a gentle easy going guy. I did see him get mad once, though. He was hunkered over working on the putt-putt car which was sitting on the tracks in front of the depot (the little cars used by the maintenance workers, we called putt-putt cars, because they went putt-putt-putt down the tracks). Anyway, Big John was very intent on his work, when a train came pulling into the station. The engineer decided for a joke, he'd give the putt-putt a little bump. It wasn't much of a bump, mind you, but it was enough to throw John to the ground. It didn't hurt him, but I think this sort of thing was a real no-no. Whatever the case, John got up fuming. He started up the ladder to the cab after that engineer, who by now wasn't laughing. Fortunately for him, a bunch of bystanders grabbed John, holding him down 'til he cooled a little. The engineer apologized from the cab, but he wouldn't come down after that.

Come election time, Big John was always there to vote. Nearly everybody in the community voted, and even though it was a secret ballot, the number of voters was so small, and the election board was made up of local citizens so they knew who voted for who without even trying. (Of course I can't say that they didn't try some). Now, Big John's ballot was the easiest of all to spot. It was always entirely blank. You see Big John couldn't read or write, but he wouldn't miss his legal right to vote.

C.A.P.

Charles Arthur Phelps, I think was his name, but all I ever knew him by was Old Cap, or Cap Phelps. He was a pretty important character around Ravendale, especially by my day, since he owned most of the town by that time. This may sound like a big deal, to own a town, but as you'll see in the next chapter, it really wasn't all that noteworthy. Still, this got him the nickname of Mayor.

Cap was a big man, and a big eater, and he loved to come to our house to eat Mom's wonderful down-home southern and ranch style cooking. He also loved venison, and *poached* deer on our ranch. Well, sort of poached. The whole area was supposed to be a no hunting area according to the Fish and Game, but we were so remote that they never came out there, and we hunted whenever we pleased. But nobody ever abused the privilege that I know of.

One time when I was just a little kid, I overheard Mom telling Dad how "Old Cap eats like a hog". He kinda gobbled his food, and made a lot of noise. So I made up this song "Old Cap Eats Like a Hog" to the tune of "The Old Gray Mare" which I sang for him the next time he came to dinner. Fortunately, he was hard of hearing, and missed the whole performance.

I learned some very good things from Old Cap though. He helped out a lot around the ranch. He was a really good mechanic, and a blacksmith. He taught me a lot as I helped him run the old blacksmith's forge. He also taught me about brute strength. He and Dad and I were preparing to load a big heavy piece of culvert pipe into the back of our pickup so we could haul it somewhere for him. Old Cap, he says to me, "Now when you lift this with us, you make a big grunting noise like this. GRRRMPH. You can lift a lot more if you grunt".

I've surprised a lot of people over the years—not just because of the loud GRRRMPH when I lift something, but because I can lift things a lot bigger and heavier than people think. It really works. Try it sometime. If nothing else, it'll get you some attention.

SISTERS COULD BE CHARACTERS TOO, YOU KNOW

Every boy should have a sister. I was blessed with two (or cursed, depending on how you look at it). Linda is six years my senior, and Leanna is five years older than me. In the beginning I wasn't aware that they were different from most girls. Tomboyish, they were. In fact, they were the most tomboyish girls I ever knew. They could ride horses and work cattle, or work in the hayfields, or do any man's work just as good as anybody. And if you crossed them, they could slug you so hard you'd think you were kicked by a mule. They used to threaten "I'll knock your head to a peak, and then knock the peak off". And they meant it too!

Even before the age of remembering, my sisters started to toughen me up for life. The story goes that shortly after my birth, my sister Leanna was playing house, with me being *her baby*. She would have been five at the time. She took me upstairs where she made a bed for me right at the top of the stairs. Naturally, the first thing I did was to roll myself down the stairs, thump, thump, bump, all the way to the bottom. I don't know if that knocked my brains out or if maybe it knocked what little sense I do have into my head, but that was the start of my life.

I have this one particular scar. How sweet revenge can be. (Let me explain) I had plenty of fights with my sisters when we were young and there was this one particular fight between Leanna and me. I think we'd argue today about what the fight was about. But one thing's sure, there was a fight, and since this is my story, I'll tell it my way. I say we were arguing over some Christmas candy. She said it was hers. I had it, and I said it was mine. Now my sister Leanna isn't long on words, but quick to act, so she hauled off and punched me a good one. (She says she only shoved me a little), but whatever, I got knocked for a loop, falling back and hitting my head on the corner of the piano, cutting a little gash in the back of my head. Mind you now, it wasn't much of a wound, but it bled so wonderfully. Blood ran down my neck, and back and onto the living room floor. I've bled a-plenty in my life, and so this didn't really scare me, but it sure gave me a great opportunity to make a lot of noise, get some sympathy, and get my sister in trouble.

Over time, I grew bigger, and tougher, and at one point, I actually thought I'd got to where I could whup my sisters. I decided on Linda first. I was sure that if I got in the first punch, and hit her as hard as I could, I'd get the best of her. I planned it for days—even weeks, then at the first opportunity for a fight, I rared back, hauled off, and punched her right in the stomach just as hard as I could. She just looked me right in the eye, and started laughing. I knew then, I was one dead kid. That was the last illusion I had of being able to whup my sisters.

Thank God for sisters. Mine are the greatest. They set (mostly) good examples for me, and taught me a lot of good things, beyond how to defend myself. They are to this day, wonderful friends.

My experience with sisters didn't teach me much about the proper way to treat a girl, and one time on a gradeschool outing, I was maybe 8 or 9 at the time. We were at a sheep shearing, and a bunch of us kids were playing king of the mountain on a stack of filled wool sacks. Wool sacks are very large burlap bags, and when stuffed with wool, they are then stacked up like a huge log pile. They are of course much softer than logs, and great for playing on. Anyhow, at one point, the Gilliland girl and I got in a disagreement about something or other, and I bopped her on the nose. I got in a lot of trouble over that. Mrs. Gould, our teacher gave me a big lecture on how little boys weren't supposed to give little girls nosebleeds. All I knew was that she was as big as I was, and I hit her before she could hit me. I figgered all girls were like my sisters, and I better protect myself. If she'd been smaller than me, it would have been different. You didn't hit someone smaller than you. That was the "rule". Unless, of course it was your younger brother, then it was ok. At least that's what my sisters thought, and when my younger brother came along I maintained the same rule. I'm sure glad that when my kid brother grew up, and got way bigger than me, he had a very forgiving heart. He's now my bestest male friend.

I learned another good lesson one time when my family was visiting at the Crabtree's Ranch across the Plains. Chap and Caesar (Crabtree) had the greatest barn on the Plains. It was a big barn with a loft and we were playing out around the barn—my sisters and I and another kid named Bobby Dummitt. Bobby was about the same age as me, probably about 6 at the time. Anyhow, he got to bragging how tough he was 'cause he could smoke cigarettes. This made my sisters mad. They thought smoking was stupid. So they decided they'd show Bobby how to *really* be tough. They locked him and me in the barn, and told him if he really thought he was tough he'd prove it by jumping out of the loft. So we climbed up into the loft to check it out. Boy, was it a long way down. The girls were down on the ground, and they kept goading Bobby, trying to get him to jump out and kill himself (I think). Well, he was pretty smart, and he wasn't about to jump, even though they told him he would stay there 'til he starved if he didn't. So next, they started trying to shame him by calling him a sissy. Nothing was worse than being called a sissy, unless it was being called a dude. Nothing worked. So now they started in taunting him, saying that I would jump out, that I was littler than him, and that I wasn't no sissy. This went on for awhile, but didn't work either. Pretty soon it became apparent to me that I was going to have to jump or be labeled a sissy. I was proud that my sisters would say that I wasn't no sissy, but it sure looked like a long way down. I figured it might kill me, but yet it wouldn't be worth living if I had to be called a sissy. Tough decision! I finally mustered up all my courage and out of the barn loft I went. Down, down, down I went. First, my feet hit the ground. Then, my legs crumpled and, my knees and chin came together like two freight trains. Stars were everywhere. The girls were saying "See, Johnny's no sissy. Come on, sissy Bobby, jump. Johnny's not hurt, are you?" I just gritted my teeth, grinned, and tried to hold back the tears. I couldn't say a word, what with the wind knocked plumb out of me. So, Bobby didn't jump, I didn't die, and I wasn't no *sissy*. A big *sucker*? Yep!

It's A Long Way Down

A VERY HOT LAVA ROCK

In addition to sisters, everybody oughta have a brother too. I have one—Don. To say *eccentric character*, is to be redundant. Don is a doubly eccentric character, which is redundant redundant! He had a passion and love for the work of the cowboy, and up until he ruptured a disk in his back, he was one of the best. He was and is a rambunctious type, and thus provided me with some of the best stories in this book.

For example, Donald and our Dad were riding one very chilly fall day up on the mountain. They had packed a lunch as they planned to be out all day. So when noontime came they dismounted, and made a circle of lava rocks to contain a little campfire, to warm the lunch, and the body. Now as it happens, there is a certain type of lava rock that when it gets hot, it explodes. I don't know if there is anyway to spot one of these rocks until it just blows up. Oh, I don't mean it explodes like a bomb, but just pops with a loud bang and flies into pieces. And such was the case on this day. One of the lava rocks burst, throwing little pieces of hot lava shrapnel all over the place, one of which just happened to drop down the front of Don's shirt. Natural instinct prevailed and he slapped his hand to his chest and caught it inside his shirt. Of course, it burned right away so he dropped loose of it, and it fell a little further down his chest, and he grabbed it again. And so on 'til it gets down pretty close to uh . . . . to uh . . . how am I gonna say this in a G rated fashion? Let's say it was getting too close to the family jewels. Well, you get the picture. Anyhow, this time he held tight onto that hot little bugger 'til it cooled down. He carries the scars of that little mishap down his frontside to this day.

Catch That Hot Lava Rock

LOOK OUT FOR THE ONE ARMED BANDIT

Even though Dad was born at the beginning of the twentieth century, the Plains and its people were sorta stuck in the 19th century. It is a fact that some of us from that area of the world still haven't fully got away from pioneer thinking.

In the late 1960s Dad got himself elected to the County Board of Supervisors, and he actually started to have a little income, and a little money to spend on things. Us kids were all about raised and gone, and with the small salary he was now getting he began to have a change of lifestyle. Like he traded the old pickup off for a four-wheel-drive truck, and did a lot of fixing up around the ranch. Then one day the Board of Supervisors made a trip to Reno, Nevada for a convention.

Although we'd been to Reno a few times, it had been for business and not the night life. So when the other Supervisors finally goaded Dad into spending a little of his newly earned money to play a slot machine, Dad was in for an entirely new experience. He was standing there putting quarters in a one armed bandit and pulling the handle when all of a sudden lights started flashing, bells started ringing, and money started falling out and onto the floor. Dad, he took off like a scared Jackrabbit—thought he'd busted the darn thing. Finally, one of the change girls caught up with him and explained he'd just won a jackpot.

Some people called us ignorant. Dad was only educated to the 8th grade. Grandpa probably never went to school at all. But the pioneers and homesteaders knew more about this mother earth and the way she operates than anybody who went to school for a lifetime, but never actually scratched around in the dirt to survive. We were educated all right, but it didn't all come from book-learnin'. In fact the best education never came from inside the walls of a school at all. That's my fillyossify.

We weren't, however, as ignorant about modern things as many *civilized* people thought. We were just cautious. Considering all the social, economic, and political challenges facing us today, maybe we—and *civilized* people too—should have been more cautious about modernizing. It changes the way people think, and it changes the way they treat each other. And it ain't, in all cases, for the better.

R RATED STORY (BY SOME STANDARDS, ANYHOW)

In 1970, we located some of Dad's long lost cousins in the Basque Country of Spain. It was decided that us kids would treat Dad and Mom to a trip over there to meet them. Dad, like all of us, was not a big time traveler. "I've been all the way to Reno", he'd say when people were talking about traveling. He liked to read a lot though, and knew a lot about the world from that. He was fluent in the Basque language, and you could say he spoke real good American (English), but he didn't know a single word of French, or German, and only a few cusswords in Spanish. And Mom, she only speaks "Arkie" (Southern American). So as you might imagine, when they were traveling through Germany, and France by train, they were in for some interesting experiences.

They were spending the night in a hotel room somewhere in France, and Dad always liking to have something to read went out for a walk to see if he could find a newspaper or something in English. After awhile, he came back with a magazine that he had found, and he set it down on the nightstand. While he was taking a bath and getting ready for bed, Mom picked up the magazine, and started to browse through it. Pretty soon she says to Dad, "Do you know what you've got here"?

"No," he says, "I haven't looked at it, but it was the only thing I could find in English."

He'd never seen a Playboy Magazine before in his life. Neither had Mom. She wasn't impressed. Dad didn't do any reading that night.

4

SO YOU THINK YOUR
HOME TOWN WAS SMALL?

RAVENDALE

I guess I have to claim Ravendale as my home town, though I never lived there. In fact, up until I got shipped off to the city of Susanville to go to High School, I never lived in a town at all. Our ranch was six miles east of Ravendale, so if anybody ever asked where we were from we always said Ravendale. Of the three towns on the Plains, Ravendale was medium size. Even considering that, you would probably consider it to be a small town. I'm probably the only guy you'll ever know—that is of course, if you ever get a chance to know me—who can draw you a map of every street in his hometown, (There was only one crossroad) and who can tell you the name every person who lived there, as well as the names of their dogs and cats. The population stayed pretty much around twenty in my day. We used to joke about both city limit signs, "Entering", and "leaving", being on the same post—or how if you blinked your eyes as you drove through, you'd miss the town altogether. The town consisted mainly of the one business, (gas station, café, and bar combined), the railroad depot, the county road department, a post office, various homes, and on the hill above town was the old one room schoolhouse. To the south of town was the railroad pumphouse and the gigantic water tank for watering up the steam locomotives.

The Southern Pacific Railroad was the heart and soul of the town. Most of the people who lived in town, were associated with the railroad. The depot, the section gang workers, the pumping station, even the cafe existed mainly for feeding the train crews. The old steam engines that still ran on the Southern Pacific line from Reno, Nevada, to Alturas, California, had to water up frequently and so there were a lot of little towns along the line up until the late 1950s when they finally began to convert their locomotives from coal power to diesel. I got acquainted with Ravendale when I began gradeschool. Pep (Steven) Mayfield, whose father, John, ran the depot, was the same age as myself, and we became pals. We started gradeschool together, and finished together. Most of the time it was just the two of us in our grade. (All eight grades attended school in the one room school) The number of kids at school during the eight years that I attended, varied from ten to fifteen students.

Since Pep's dad was the head operator for the railroad, his family lived in the depot house. Being Pep's buddy, I naturally spent a lot of time around the railroad. I remember watching John operate the telegraph, and wondering how he knew what it was saying. Clickety, clickety, click, I couldn't tell the dits from the dahs. (Morse code spelled out words in dots and dashes.) Sometimes John would get a message on the telegraph for an incoming train, and he would write it up on a little piece of paper. Then, he had this special delivery system which was a long stick with a broad fork on one end. The note would be carefully folded, twisted into a long string which was then fastened between the forks. Then when the train came roaring down the line, John would go out on the dock, hold up the stick, and as the engine came flying through, the engineer would stick his arm out the window of the cab, and hook the string and message from the forks, thus getting his new orders. I never saw them miss the message, though I always expected them to. I really loved those steam engines—and feared them too. Like some mythical dragon, roaring and belching smoke and steam, whistling, clanging, and chugging. Mysterious! Monstrous! Even when sitting idle they were always chugging, clanking, and hissing. You never knew but what it might just roar to life, jump off the tracks and come chasing after you. And when they really did take off down the tracks, there was such a roar and blast of steam and smoke, and bell-ringing, and whistling, snorting and chugging, you just knew you better not ever turn your back on one of them. I had not the slightest idea how a steam engine worked. But I was terribly fascinated by all the working parts—all located right on the surface where you could watch them work. Pipes, valves, domes, bells,—and those wonderful drive arms, and steam valve levers working back and forth, up and down, and round and round. The sights, the sounds, and the smells are burned into my memory forever.

TERMO

Have you ever noticed how people who are from a small town really like to brag about how small their hometown was. Well, you probably never heard of Termo. Ravendale was at the south end of the Plains, and Madeline was to the north. Termo was right in the middle. I remember once when I was in gradeschool, a family moved into the town of Termo—and *doubled the population of the town!*

The normal population of Termo in those days was two and one half. Yep it's true. The owners of the only business, Sulo and Ida Lakso lived there year 'round, and Pete Oldershaw stayed in a little cabin during the summers and went south during the winter. Everybody thought Pete was a bit of a dude, or flatlander, as we called folks who weren't of the hardy pioneer stock. Maybe he was smarter though. It took me a long time to get smart enough to figure out I could get away from those long cold winters.

Awhile back, I heard that the town of Termo is for sale. Just think! you could own your own town. You could own the post office, you could own the only business, which would be whatever you wanted it to be, and declare yourself mayor, or king, or whatever you wanted to be.

Hey! if you don't believe that these little town exist, get a 3-A map of northeastern California. You'll see 'em all right. If you look hard enough around Ravendale, you'll even see a little road with the Basko name of Garate on it. That's where my Grandpa and Dad homesteaded. It really ain't nothin' to brag about—just a fact.

5

COLD COLD COLD PLAINS

30 BELOW ZERO

Having a big pile of stove wood on hand by fall was not an option on the Plains. The only source of heat was the wood stove, and the old house wasn't insulated. It had no foundation—just sat on short posts on flat rocks. Over the years it had settled here and there and gaps developed around the windows and doors which let the bone freezing north wind blow the cold and snow right into the house. It wasn't unusual to get up in the morning and have ice on the inside of the windows, and have to sweep out the snow that blew in over the night. The stove wood we used was juniper and mountain mahogany which warmed you twice. Once when you cut it with axes and the old crosscut saw, and then again when you burned it in the stove in the winter time—that is, if the north wind didn't blow—in which case nothin' could warm you.

I know! Right now you're probably thinkin' "This guy is blowin' smoke. This is Sunny California he's talkin' about". Well, I won't try too hard to convince you, but if you take a look at a map you'll see that California is one big state—bigger than some countries, and there is enough room there for every kind of climate. On the Plains at 5,200 ft. elevation, the winters were *cold*! Many times we'd go to bed all our clothes on, including coats. (We did take our boots off.) We slept in twos. I slept with my brother, and my two sisters slept together. It was a matter of survival. There were nights that I never got warm.

FROZEN BEEFSTEAKS FOR HANDS?

I remember, though somewhat painfully, as an aspiring young cowboy my first experience with buckarooing in really cold weather. Not that I hadn't experienced cold before. It can easily get down to 20 or 30 degrees below zero on a winter night on the Madeline Plains—mean north wind-a-blowing, bone freezing cold.

Anyway, back to my story. I went out to ride with the crew on the ranch where I was working. It was a really cold nasty morning. In addition to Levis, wool shirt, Levi jacket, and a hat, the tough older cowboys might add a second shirt and some flannel underwear on a really cold day. I dressed the same—didn't want to be pegged as a sissy or dude, you know.

Right away my ears began to hurt. My hands and feet began to ache. And then I really began to hurt. I couldn't let on of course. The cold didn't seem to be bothering anybody else. I gritted my teeth, and steeled with all my might against the cold. Eventually I was finally numb all over. But even when you go numb with cold, it still hurts—kinda like when you swat your thumb with a hammer—after a while it settles down to that deep throbbing ache. Except that with the cold it is all over your whole body.

After what seemed like an eternity noon came, and we headed for the ranch house for dinner. That was the noon meal—*dinner*. It *was* the big meal of the day. We got to the ranch, and unsaddled our horses. I noticed right away that my hands seemed like a couple of dead foreign objects attached to my wrists. The fingers just refused to respond to any command from my somewhat also frozen brain.

When we got inside the house, the missus of the ranch had a blazing fire going which I expected would feel really good. The trouble is that warming up in any way other than really slow, makes you hurt even worse. The next thing I began to notice quite intensely, was that I hadn't gone *number one* for about 5 hours. (Is that ok for a G rating?) I mean, who wants to get out of the saddle when it's 20 below, and the wind howlin' like a banshee, to do that little chore. The things on your hands were more like icicles than fingers. Can you imagine touching yourself *down there* with icicles. Brrr—shiver shiver!

Anyway, when the warm air hit me, I really started to squirm, and excused myself to go outside to relieve myself. The problem was that with the two frozen clubs on the ends of my wrists, I couldn't undo the buttons on my Levis.

So there I was—standing outside the corner of the house, squirming and fidgeting, about to fill my boots down my pantleg, when out comes the missus to see what's keeping me. She saw right away what my problem was, and came over and says to me, "Here, let me unbutton those for you, I do it for the guys all the time". My protests came out pretty weak. I just wanted to get the job over with. So she *did*—unbutton my Levis that is. And I *did* get the job done. I sure hoped no one was watching my embarrassment—even if the missus *was* my mother, and even if I *was* only six years old.

LOST IN A SNOWSTORM

It started on a school day. It was snowing that morning when Mom drove us to school in Ravendale, six miles from the ranch. It snowed all day. (The year was 1952 and it was March. When the storm ended it had dumped at least 5 feet of snow.) When Mom and Dad started out to pick us up from school, they got the old pickup stuck at the windmill about a mile and a half from the house. Dad walked back home, harnessed up Smitty and Britches, our team of work horses, came back and pulled the pickup loose from the snowdrift. Ain't it something, now, how two real horses could unloose a machine worth supposedly 50 or 60 horsepower. Anyway, they left the team at the windmill, and came on and picked us up. But then on the way home we got stuck in the snow again, when we were about three miles from home. So Dad walked to the windmill to get the team, and try to pull us out again. But this time we were really stuck. Try as they might, old Smitty and Britches just couldn't get us free. They pulled and jerked so hard they broke the double-tree. (Part of the hitching apparatus.) The snow was just too deep.

A decision was made. Dad, and my two sisters, Linda age 12, and Leanna age 11 would take the team and slog their way through the snow to the ranch, where, as always, there was livestock waiting to be fed and watered. Mom and I and my younger brother, Don, age one and a half, would walk back to the Morgan's place, about a half mile behind us, using the tracks made in the snow by the pickup as our guide. You have to realize that when it's snowing a blizzard like that you can't see anything but white. It is impossible to tell direction, and it is very easy to become confused and lost. So anyway, we separated and headed off for our destinations. We made it to the Morgan's house without much difficulty, and there we sat with them, waiting for the old crank phone to ring to tell us that Dad and the girls were safely home. We waited, and waited, and waited. Mom was getting quite nervous. It is so easy for the imagination to run away at a time like that, and the situation *was* truly perilous. Finally after what seemed an eternity, the old phone jangled. Dad and the girls were safely home. What a relief! The fact was, though that they *had* gotten lost, and except for a miracle, they would have died.

The events went like this. After leaving the pickup, they had followed the road as far as the windmill. In spite of the heavy snow and wind, they had been able to make out the boundaries of the road by the fences which bordered it. Leanna was getting tired, and kept wanting to lay down in the snow and go to sleep. In those days we didn't know the word hypothermia, but we knew if someone got cold and went to sleep in the snow, they would never wake up. So Dad, in his anxiety to get home, decided to cut catty-corner across the field at the windmill, rather than following the longer route along the road. He knew that by giving the horses their head, they would head for the barn. What he hadn't figured on was that he kept falling in the deep snow, and each time he fell, naturally the lines were given a yank, and apparently the horses got confused. At any rate, after what seemed like forever, they came upon of the fence that runs east and west by the house. By this time, the fence was nearly buried in the snow, but since they had obviously missed the house, all they had to do was follow it to the house. But now, the life and death question for Dad. Did he follow the fence to the left as his gut instincts told him or go to the right. Linda was only 12, but she said she thought they should go to the right. That was *her* gut instinct. For some reason, Dad finally decided to go with Linda's suggestion, though it was one of the hardest choices he ever made. He was a man of decision, as were all the pioneers, and for some unknown reason, this time he chose to go with the decision of a child. To this day Linda has no idea why she felt they should go to the right, or how she was able to convince Dad. But she was correct in her feeling, as is obvious, because they all survived.

It can be nothing short of a miracle. They could have crossed over the fence in a deep drift, and never seen it. They could have done the usual thing and simply gone with Dad's instinct. They were probably only about a quarter of a mile from the house, but in the blizzard you were lucky to see something 20 feet away.

The next day the storm let up some, and Tom Morgan, by use of the county road grader, managed to get Mom, me and my brother, as well as our old pickup, safely home. But by the end of that second day, the snow had blown and drifted so deep that everyone on the Plains was snowed in. A schoolboy's dream—being snowed in and no way to go to school. It was a rancher's nightmare. Cattle to be fed and watered, spring grasses more than a month away, and haystacks nearly gone. We had to tunnel our way oug of the snow to get out of the house. We used the work horses to beat down trails through the snow to the haystack, to the starving cattle, to the watering troughs, and to the outbuildings.

THE ONE AND ONLY EASY CATTLE DRIVE

We were, during this big snow of 1952, fully pre-occupied with trying to save the cattle. The Jackrabbits had started their spring breeding, and they too had nothing to eat. It was a matter of days until the starving rabbits and livestock had devoured the last remaining haystack—the last straw, literally. It would be weeks before the first blades of grass would peek through the melting snow.

By our good fortune, the old crank phone had held together through all this, and we were able to communicate with our neighbors. The County road department had linked two huge D8 bulldozers together, and were gradually punching trails through the snow to the various ranches, and haystacks. So we got them to come and punch a road out from our place to the Madeline Ranch, three miles east of us where there was a haystack we had arranged to use. We rounded up our cattle, and put them in the road behind those two big dozers, and off we went. There was no place for the cows to go but right down the road, the snow being piled in a sheer wall on either side, as high as a man's head when he was mounted up. That was the only easy cattle drive I was ever on.

6

MUSTANGS AND OTHER
HORSE TYPE CRITTERS

PEANUT

Growing up and living on a cattle ranch meant you rode horses a lot. Sometimes it seemed like that is all you did, and always you were behind a bunch of cows and calves that you were supposed to make go somewhere they didn't want to go. I was riding alone in the saddle working cattle by the ripe old age of three. Before that I had only been in the saddle with my mom. I started on old Patches, an old Pinto cow horse who knew how to work cattle. He was old and a little tired, and often would fall asleep and just stand there. My job at that time was to give him a kick to wake him up so he could go back to doing his part of the job.

I don't remember much about my early days in the saddle. What I do remember is long hot dusty days in the saddle, and long shivering freezing cold days in the saddle, day after day after day. And little calves that just wanted to lay down and rest, and cows that wanted to stop and eat grass, or turn back, looking for their calves that had become separated from them. You'd yell and holler 'til you'd go hoarse trying to keep 'em moving. It was hard grueling work, not exactly the romantic thing you see depicted in the movies. By the time I was ten or so, I could tell a yearling heifer from a steer, and I could tell the first calf heifers from the older cows, and so on. By this time I was good enough at it not to hate it anymore, though I can't say I ever did come to *love* buckarooing.

After I outgrew old Patches, Peanut became my horse. Peanut was a mustang, a breed of wild horses that range throughout various parts of the west. Not a large horse, the mustang is of mixed colors, and usually not super intelligent, and often inbred. But they are very hardy, and well suited for the rugged life in the rough, rocky, brushy kind of mountains that surround the Madeline Plains. Peanut, white in color, wasn't a bad looking horse, but was super-typical of the mustangs—crazy as a bedbug. His first owners had tried to train him as a racehorse, and he never got over thinkin' he was a racehorse. He never, in all his many years on the ranch, gained a lick of sense about working cattle. This meant that you had to show him every move, which turns into a lot of work. In spite of all his failings, Peanut was my horse, and I came to love him. I worked real hard with him and gained his trust, and eventually we became a pretty good team. We shared one thing in common, for sure, in that neither of us cared a whole heck-of-a lot for working cattle. It was simply a job, and certainly not an easy one.

PEANUT—SMART IF HE WANTED TO BE

I really shouldn't say that Peanut never learned anything about working cattle. He did learn *one* thing. One day we were moving a bunch of cows, and we were having trouble with this one old cow. Time after time, we would find her lagging behind the rest of the herd. We'd go and get behind her, and I'd yell, and holler, and finally she'd amble on up to the herd. Next thing you know, though, there she was lagging behind again. Peanut and I were really getting frustrated with this old bag of bovine bones. I was at my wits end when finally old Peanut had the first (and only?) idea of his life. We got up behind her and he reached out and gave her a hard bite on the rump. With that, she took off like a bolt of lighting. We had no more trouble with that old cow after that, and Peanut had learned a really good skill which he seemed to really enjoy using ever after. He was the only *biting* cow horse I ever knew.

PEANUT COULD STOP ON A DIME

Peanut was scared to death of anything out of the ordinary. He'd spook and jump out of his skin at the slightest thing—or at nothing at all. You never went to sleep on Peanut. You never knew when he'd spook and leave you sitting on air.

Dad and I were moving a bunch of cows to the homestead one day. The "homestead" was a section (640 acres) of land on Spanish Springs Peak that Dad homesteaded in 1931. The original homestead, which Grandpa took out and where our house sat was just called "home", or "the house". Anyway we were moving this herd, driving them along the Madeline Ranch road, which ran east from the house. At this one point, we had to turn the cows off the road and head them south up the mountain.

Peanut—One Spook Of A Mustiang

Just at the right time Dad told me to get up in front of the cows and turn them, so Peanut and I got off the road to the left, and started clipping along so as to get around the string of cows. The cows were feeling pretty frisky, and started to run too. The faster we'd go, the faster they'd go, and by the time we finally got in front of the herd, Peanut was at a full gallop—nothing unusual about that. Peanut loved to run—and cows would always dis-co-operate. The unusual thing arose when we got back on the road. We were still wound up in a full gallop, when suddenly I saw it—right there in the road directly in front of us. Some winter erosion had left a drainage culvert exposed—a bright shiny strip across the road. Now, old Peanut was predictable too, in a situation like this, and I knew exactly what he was going to do, but it all happened too fast to take evasive action. My nerves steeled, fully expecting to be scraping up the earth with my chin in the next instant. Peanut did just what I knew he would, slamming all four feet, he jerked to a dead stop. I thought that was what I would be too—*dead*, that is. I sailed up and over the saddle horn, but by some strange stroke of luck, I came to rest at the back of Peanut's head, my legs wrapped firmly around his neck, his ears sticking out either side of my groin, and myself hanging down over his head so I was looking back into his face, eyeball to eyeball. I very quickly slithered back down his neck, back over the horn and into the saddle, very shaken, but unhurt, and for once, *VERY* glad to be in the saddle.

FAREWELL OLD PEANUT (I get a little sentimental)

I never was really crazy about riding. It was mostly a job at which I got pretty good out of necessity. I don't know if there is a horse heaven or not, but if there is, I hope when I cross over the Great Divide, I get to visit there and see my special friend, Old Peanut. And I'd like to meet Dad too and go riding one more time. Dad's been dead since 1988.

7

CRAZY NON-EQUESTRIAN CRITTERS

THE COWBOY, THE KID, AND THE COYOTE

Gross rated description:
For the most part, the coyote didn't cause us serous problems—mostly just a nuisance. Like, at times, we couldn't keep cats around, because the coyotes loved to eat 'em. The chickens, without fail, had to be locked up at night. But it was the occasional killer that really gave the coyote a bad name. Every now and then, there would be a coyote that would go to killing for sport. He'd go through a band of sheep at night and kill every sheep he could get his teeth into, and just leave them lie. He'd kill your dog, your cats, and any small game, not because he was hungry, but just for the fun of killing. If he could find a young calf, unprotected by it's mother, that was fair game. The coyote is super smart, and worst of all, in my mind, is when a coyote waits for the calf to nurse and have a stomach full of milk. The coyote will get the calf down, rip open its stomach, and drink the milk then go off leaving the calf to die. Maybe coyotes can get The Great White Hunter Syndrome. (See Ch. 20)

Now back to the G rated story
My brother Don, fresh out of college, and newly married, was managing the Elmer Williams ranch out of Termo. A young friend of his, Bob Crabtree, was out of school for Christmas vacation and was staying with Don and his wife, helping with feeding the cattle. There was several inches of snow on the ground, and for several days, a coyote had been killing calves for the fresh milk, (See gross rated description above if you dare.) and on one particular afternoon, Don and Bob were heading for Termo in the pickup. As they passed the feedground, they happened to spot the

25

coyote after a calf. They screeched to a stop, and Don jumped out with the 30-30 rifle he carried and the coyote took off into the brush. She was of course running away from them, out of sight in the sagebrush, but there was a levee on the far side of the feedground, and Don, knowing she would have to go up over the dike, aimed in the general direction of where she seemed to be heading. Sure enough, she popped up onto the dike, and Don squeezed off a shot, the only bullet he had with him. The coyote collapsed in a heap, and slid out of sight on the far side of the dike.

Don and Bob headed over to where she had disappeared to see if they had killed her, and when they came up over the dyke, there she was, lying in a heap, looking pretty dead. However, she was either stunned, or playing dead which a coyote will do. When they came up over the dike, she suddenly came quite to life, full of hate and revenge. Normally a coyote will steer clear of humans, but when they are wounded, or cornered, they are quite willing to attack a human. Such was the case here, and Bob being the smaller of the two was the logical target. Bob seeing the danger, took off in a dead run. As the coyote shot past my brother hot after Bob, he being a man and Bob being a kid, Don knew he had to do something. With no time to think, he did the only thing possible. As the coyote flew by, he jumped behind her and grabbed her by the tail. There she was pawing and clawing and churning the ground. When she finally realized she wasn't going anywhere, that something was holding her back, she turned her head to see what was going on. Now, of course, Don became the new target. Knowing full well that you can't outrun a coyote, what to do now? No time to think, he instinctively began spinning around in circles, swinging the coyote by the tail, the centrifugal force barely keeping her from being able to get her teeth in him, all the while yelling for Bob to come back and help. Fortunately, Bob had the courage and self reliance of his pioneer parentage, and fortunately he got his composure, and fortunately he was able to find a piece of old broken fence post with which he came back and whopped Mrs. coyote over the head.

Once in a while things work out for the best. In this case, even the calf that the coyote had been after wasn't seriously injured, and with a little doctoring, he was good as new in no time.

A Coyote By The Tail

MEL THE REAL HERO

The problem with water is that on the Madeline Plains there just simply ain't much of it. What there was, was mainly for drinkin'—and the occasional bath. For sure there wasn't a lot of swimming that went on—especially among my Dad's side of the family. We all had some kind of natural fear of gettin' in the water. Now, Mom's side of the family was different. They had migrated to California from Arkansas, and they were all as natural in the water as a fish in the sea. My two sisters somehow followed in the tradition of the Arkie side of the family, and loved to swim.

Mel, our ever faithful part Collie cow dog followed in the traditions of Dad's family, and wanted nothing to do with getting in the water. There were just a few places on the Plains where there were springs, and usually ponds had been built to hold water for livestock. And it was to such a place we went on one very hot summer day. We headed off to the south of Ravendale to the Bingham reservoir for a *swim*. When we got there, my two sisters were already in their swim suits, and anxious to get in the water, they went on ahead, up over the dam and out of our sight into the middle of the pond. Next was good old Mel. When he came up over the dam, and saw the two girls out in the water, screechin' and splashin' and playin' in the water, he thought they were drowning. He went into utter hysteria. First, he'd wade out into the water a little bit, wanting to go out and save the girls, but then his fear of the water would get the best of him, and he'd run back to where the rest of us were, barking franticly, begging us to come and help. Then, he'd run back to the water again, and try to go out in the water. He just couldn't make himself do it, and back again he'd come to us begging for help. He just couldn't be consoled, so finally, Mom made the girls come out of the water so he could see they were OK. He jumped all over them, and practically licked them to death, he was so happy to see them safe on dry ground.

It just ain't fully possible for me to say how special Old Mel was. One time he and a half grown pup we had acquired, were roaming way off down near where the haystack was in the lower field, and Mel caught and killed a Jackrabbit. Of course Mel didn't know we were watching from the house as he gave the rabbit to the pup to bring home. Across the field they came, the pup with the rabbit, and Mel at his side. He was willing to let the pup do the work of draggin' it home, but wasn't about to let him have credit for the kill. For show and tell in front of his family, just before they got to the house, Mel took the rabbit away from the pup and strutted up to the house to show us his fine kill. I think for that short moment, he had a touch of the Great White Hunter Syndrome. (See Chapter 20)

Mel was a natural herder as his Collie bloodline would dictate. One summer we were running Darlene the milk cow in the lower field below the house. And Mel, completely on his own idea one late afternoon went down into the field and herded Darlene home for milking. And he did that every day for the rest of that summer.

Our dogs and cats weren't house pets. Mel never came in the house—except once on a cold wintry Christmas Eve. Us kids were playing and laughing and making a lot of noise, when we heard this scratching at the door. Mom went to see what was going on and there stood Mel, looking all forlorn and lonely. She opened the door and invited him in, and he came into the living room where the family was, laid down and watched us for a while, then went to the door to be let out, as happy as a dog could be, never to ask to come in again.

POOR LITTLE SCARED WATER SNAKE

At Ryepatch in the mountains further to the south of Ravendale is another spring and water hole. It is here we went on another one of them hot summer days—Mom, and I and my brother so Mom could have a swim. We were out on a raft in the middle of the water. Don and I were feeling fairly secure sitting on the raft. Mom was out in the water, thoroughly enjoying herself, just treading water, and relaxing. Suddenly, this little water snake came swimming up from behind her. Now for every bit us menfolk were afraid of water, my Mom was equally afraid of snakes. In Arkansas where Mom was raised there was this deadly snake called a water moccasin, which would sometimes be in the water. Anyhow, this was just a harmless little water snake. He swam up behind her, and set his head right on her shoulder to take a little rest. Up to this point, she hadn't seen him, but I was watching with great anxiety, hoping the snake would go away. I was afraid Mom would panic and drown, and I knew there would be nothing my brother and I could do to save her. Well, the little snake was having a nice rest with his head right there on her shoulder. Feeling that I had better do something, I finally said very timidly, "Mom, there's a snake", pointing at him. She looked down, and the little snake looked up. For one endless moment they just looked at each other, eyeball to eyeball. Then Mom let out this bloodcurdling scream, and then I just knew she was going to drown. The poor little snake was so scared, he couldn't turn around and get out of there fast enough. He was long gone, when Mom let out another horrific scream. In my terrified mind, I could see her drowning. Fortunately though, she was completely at home in the water, and there was no real danger of her drowning. I think she could have died of fright though. After the second banshee scream, she swam right over and got onto the raft. I asked her why she screamed the second time, after the snake was long gone. She said she didn't know—just couldn't help herself.

KILL DEER—OOPS! I MEAN KILLDEER

The killdeer is a small bird that lives on the Plains around any spring. If you got close to a nest where there were eggs, or babies, one of the parent birds would get out in front of you and start cryin' real loud, *kill-deer, kill-deer,* limping around and dragging one wing on the ground like as if it was hurt real bad. Naturally, you were curious, and wanted to get a closer look, so you headed for the decoy. But as soon as you got close, she'd gimp away, squawkin' and draggin' that wing, staying just out of your reach. Then, when she had you safely led away from her nest, she'd have a miraculous healing, spring into the air and fly away, far out of your sight before no doubt returning to her nest.

I learned that if you observed very carefully which way a kill-deer was trying to lead you, you could search very diligently in the opposite direction, and maybe find the nest. I succeeded a couple of times, and got to see the babies. They were the cutest little things I ever did see. They had a body that looked like a little round cottonball, with two toothpick-like legs. And another, shorter toothpick for a neck, and for a head, a teeny cottonball with a little speck of a beak, and two big black eyes. If ever there was a critter, human or animal, that could touch you right in the heart to never hurt innocent youngsters, it would be the baby killdeer.

8

WORK IS FUN?

CUT FIREWOOD OR FREEZE

Dad was dedicated to his work and so was Mom. But Mom had a special gift. She actually enjoyed working. For her, working was fun, and by some kind of osmosis or something, she passed that gift on to all her kids, and even some of the neighbors' kids.

For me, woodcutting was one of the most fun jobs we did on the ranch. We used the team and wagon to go up the mountain and cut mahogany and Juniper trees. This was an old light freight wagon, much like the covered wagons, but without the cover. It had iron tires and no springs except a couple of leaf springs under the drivers seat which was a wooden seat—without any cushions.

The road up the mountain was just a couple of ruts, the result of driving the wagon up and down the mountain over a period of many years. It was rocky and rough, and the old iron tires bounced and jolted over every rock and bump, rattling you clear to the bone if you were sitting in back of the wagon or even if you were sitting on the driver's seat. When we were kids, we had this game we played in the back of the wagon. It was no good to try to sit on the bed of the wagon, because it was just too painful on the old *sit down*, (That's polite cowboy talk for butt) so what we'd do, is we'd try to stand up all the way up the mountain. The deal was, you weren't allowed to grab onto anything to help keep your balance—just stand there and kinda dance around trying not to fall down. There wasn't any win or lose in this game. The winning came in not having to sit on the hard bed, and it was a pretty good plan so long as you didn't get pitched clear out of the wagon, which did happen now and then.

One thing I'll tell you for sure, I know why in the pictures of the pioneers, you always see most of 'em walking alongside the wagon, instead of riding inside.

But now back to the wood cutting. Sometimes I would drive the team and wagon up the mountain. There was this one place where I didn't have the confidence to handle the horses. It was high up on a ridge, and the old wagon trail went through this dip, that sloped off to the canyon below. I was always afraid the wagon would tip over and go crashing down the canyon. The horses would get real nervous right there, and a lot of the time everyone but the Dad would get out of the wagon and walk around that part. One time coming home with a big pile of mahogany wood stacked up, Dad and I were in the wagon seat, and he was driving and at that particular dip, the horses got all jittery as usual, and the wagon went sideways up on two wheels, teetering over the canyon below. There it hung for what seemed an eternity—at least long enough for me to have visions of death and destruction, crashing and tumbling down the canyon in a jumble of wagon parts, horses, and mahogany logs. Well as you can plainly see, I am here to tell the story. The wagon finally settled back onto all four wheels, and we went on down the mountain. That incident never stopped us from going up the mountain for more firewood, but I never rode the wagon through that spot again and that's a fact.

(I need to tell you here, that mahogany wood really isn't mahogany. That's just what it was called. It was also called iron wood. It isn't a big tree, but heavy and hard, and really good for stove wood. I've been told by a plant expert that it is related to the rose bush.)

Wagon Load Of Winter Warmth

BRANDING—AHH, SWEET REVENGE

Maybe one reason I liked cutting fire wood is that I like to use an axe and the two man crosscut saw. Besides that, the trees are dumb and can't very often out-think you, whereas cattle are a little smarter than trees—maybe. At least they seem to be more able to defy you when you work with them. In fact sometimes it seemed that their sole purpose in life was to provide opposition in the life of a cowboy. And maybe that's why I liked branding. Branding was right next to cutting wood for fun. Usually we did it in the corral which provided a much more controlled work situation than out on the open range. You got to brand 'em and ear mark 'em, de-horn 'em, vaccinate 'em, and in case of the bull calves, make steers out of 'em. Sweet revenge, I call it. Of course it is always possible that this is the reason that cattle are so obstinate to work with when they grow up.

Gross rated explanation: To make a steer out of a bull you cut off his testicles. Well it is a little more surgical than that, but that's the simple explanation.

A FROZEN COWPIE

Sometimes the work was fun for the cowcritters, and not so fun for the cowboy. On this one particularly cold winter day, we had this sick calf out in the corral that needed some doctoring. Mom and I somehow got elected to give him a shot of penicillin. So I got my rope and Mom got the vaccine gun and bottle of medicine. I got my rope on him easy enough, but right away I lost my footing on the ice packed ground, and down I went, still holding onto the rope. The calf being a little bigger than me, and having four good feet to my two, began to drag me around the corral at full speed. I couldn't get in any position to get my footing on the icy ground, so there I was, sledding along figuring I'd just hang on and wear him down. Goodness knows I'd done that plenty of times before with other calves. So there I was, skipping over the ice on my belly when all of a sudden, wham, I run headlong right into this huge pile of frozen-solid pyramid of cow manure, knocking me loose from the rope, and halfway loose from my senses. I don't know which is worse, getting dragged through the stuff when it's green (soft), or when it's frozen hard as a rock. At any rate I saw stars for awhile.

Well, Mom and I finally got a-hold of the rope again, and got him snubbed to a fencepost. Then, I worked my way down the rope to the calf like usual, got alongside him, hunched over him and grabbed him by the flank and shoulder, and gave a big heave-ho to flip him down on his side. But again, the ice got me. My feet just couldn't get traction, and instead of me flipping the calf, I flipped myself right over his back in a somersault, landing on my back right under him, getting myself kicked and trampled. This was definitely not one of my better days. All I wanted to do was get a shot of penicillin into that critter, so he could go on livin' and makin' people miserable 'til he grew up and we sent him off to a feedlot somewhere. We finally did get that shot into him, and he did go on living, and I hope he *did* get turned into burgers and steaks for the plates of some real nice *civilized* folks off in the city somewhere.

9

INDIANS

CAPTAIN JACK (KINTPAUSH)

You've got your Hollywood version. You've got your history book version. And if you have the perseverance to find it, you can have your real version of the West and the cowboys and the Indians.

Now for myself, I lay no claim to being a historian. I don't claim to know much about the Indians, except what I know from my Indian friends. I do happen to know a couple of things that you won't find in a Hollywood movie, or in a history book, but I know them to be true. Some of the facts, I got from my brother Don. He is a true historian. He don't stop diggin' 'til he gets all the available facts and proofs before he makes a statement as fact. You wouldn't much want to make an argument with him on historical subjects, because he'd likely prove you wrong with facts.

Now you take for instance, Old Captain Jack. I never knew him. He died long before my time, but I do know some of his descendents. I've walked all over his battleground. You can do it yourself by visiting the Lavabeds National Monument in northeastern California. It is worth the visit for many reasons.

Captain Jack (Kintpuash) was a Modoc Indian, and you can read the historical versions of his life, and the Modoc War by going to the Library. You'll get the truth. That is to say you won't get any lies. But you will not get the whole story.

You see, Captain Jack led his little rag-a-tag band of fifty or so braves and a few women and children in the Modoc War, against the United States of America. Before the war was over, he was successfully holding off over a thousand US Army regulars and volunteers, and US General Canby had been killed. Before the Indians were finally defeated, the war had become a great embarrassment in Washington. Not unlike today, the question was "Why can't the mighty United States of America whup this little bunch of 'degenerate savages'"?

Well, of course, they finally were defeated and Old Captain Jack got his neck stretched, and lost his head.

Gross rated description:

It was the belief among the Modocs that if your body got dismembered you wouldn't go to the Happy Hunting Ground when you died, and so after they hanged poor Old Captain Jack *until he was dead*, they then whacked off his head. The United States wanted to make an example of Captain Jack showing what would happen to you if you defied their authority.

Now that is pretty much where the history books end. But the story goes on, and like most conflicts, never does really end. Officially, the US wanted to dramatically show the people that they had defeated this renegade. The first thing they did was have his head presented to prominent doctors in Washington DC to try to determine why, or what caused this barbarian to be such a *degenerate*. Of course, they couldn't find anything different in his brain than they would in yours or mine. Then, to make sure that the greatest possible number of people would have a chance to see how powerful the mighty US of A was, they displayed his head at various locations around the city, and finally presented his head to the Smithsonian, where it was placed on view for many years.

During the 1970's when my brother Don was researching this, he corresponded with the Smithsonian on the matter, and they were not so proud of this part of their past, and the head was at that time locked up in some deep dark basement. They even asked my brother if he had any influence with the Modocs could he possibly arrange for the Smithsonian to give the head back to them. Well, at that time it was still a very taboo issue with the Modocs. I have heard recent reports that the Smithsonian has finally been successful in returning Old Captain Jacks head to him. Leastways I reckon the Modocs put his head back with the rest of him. I hope it is true, and the Captain is finally at peace in the Happy Hunting Ground.

For me, and my experience of life, it is pretty hard to tell who is really *civilized*, and who is really a barbarian. I've known some pretty good people that have been labeled as hicks and wild cowboys. They treated the people around them a lot better that what I've seen among a lot of the so called *civilized* people.

WISDOM OF AN OLD INDIAN MAN

Many years later, in my generation, we were building a bob-wire fence between our ranch and the neighboring ranch. I was in my early teens, and ours was a family ranch, which meant we weren't big enough to hire outside help, and *we* the family, did all the work—Mom, Dad, my two sisters, my brother and me. In fact Dad used to get a little frustrated at times, and he'd tell my Mom "All I ever have to work with is women and kids. *WOMEN AND KIDS*"!

The neighbor, Percy Fredrickson, had earned big money in the construction business, and was ranching as a hobby. He was the only guy I ever knew on the Madeline Plains who had any money to speak of. So anyway, he hired help to do whatever he didn't want to do—which was most of the work. So it was, that I ended up working alongside an old Indian man who was sent by Percy to help build the fence.

Now it is my opinion that old Indian men are full of bits of all kinds of wisdom. And this old man was no exception. Anyhow he and I were building this fence up on the Spanish Springs Mountain. It was a hot, dry, dusty, typical summer. We had, on the previous day, dug holes and set all the posts, and on this particular day, were stringing and stapling up the bob-wire. I was stretching the wire with a block and tackle, and the old man was stapling it to the posts. We had worked our way pretty high up the mountain, when I happened to look way back down the way and saw a wire sagging where he had forgotten to staple it to a post.

So I says to him, "Hey look down there. You forgot to staple the wire on that post down there. See the wire saggin' down?"

"Oh no"! Says he. "I didn't forget. Only God does something perfectly. You always want to leave something undone, so as not to make God mad".

And with that, him being older and wiser, and me being younger and not so wise, guess who it was that walked back down the hill and stapled the wire on. Yep, you're right—it was me!

This might seem like a nice little joke, or that the old man was just trying to get out of some work. But really, he was speaking seriously. There really is some wisdom in what he said, and you can find it if you study on the subject long enough.

This bit of Indian wisdom could serve us all well. I use it in my music all the time. I always make sure I never play a song all the way through perfectly. (As if there was any chance of that happening. Yeah, sure!) So far as I can remember I've never had to deliberately make a mistake in playin' a song. The mistakes come to me naturally and without fail.

Not only in the field of music, but also in the *civilized* world we live and work in, people could really benefit from this little bit of wisdom. Awhile back, I made some kind of mistake in my work, and I told that little story to my boss. Somehow, he just couldn't see the wisdom (or the humor) in it. Maybe he's just too *civilized*. Ain't that a shame!?

10

FROM JUSTICE TO INJUSTICE

SETTLE YOUR DISPUTE YOUR WAY

In Grandfather's generation and partway into Dad's generation, pioneer justice played a small role on the Plains, providing some genuine common sense justice, as well as some community entertainment. People occasionally called upon officers of the law to come up to the Plains to settle disputes, and the entire community would come to see the show.

Art Anderson who went on to become the Superior Court Judge of Lassen County, had his very first right-out-of-law-school, legal case on the Madeline Plains. He told me this story, himself.

A squabble had broken out at the Ravendale bar, and during the course of events, Lee Morgan broke a pool stick over Cap Phelps' head. Now Old Cap wasn't hurt much. On the Plains, heads were usually harder than cue sticks. You had to be tough to survive in that part of the frontier. But, considering his position in the community as owner of most of the town, I guess Cap felt he had to defend his pride, and the result was a lawsuit.

On the appointed day, a judge, and a couple of lawyers, one of which was Art Anderson who had been engaged to represent one of the principals, arrived from Susanville, which was the county seat and nearest source of "civilization", some sixty miles away. A temporary courtroom was set up in the Termo dance hall, and the entire population arrived to see the performance. The trial began, and accusations were made, pleadings were called for and so on. Then the questioning began as to who did what to whom. The two contestants began to get all fired up again, and soon were beak to beak, shaking their fists, and making threats upon each other's person. The old judge, he leaped to his feet, slamming his gavel to the table in a thunderous crack, "All right, you two, if you're going to act like this, just get your carcasses outside and settle it your way". And that's exactly what they did. End of Case.

Says Art, "I never studied anything in all my years of law school to prepare me for something like this".

GOOD WHISKY?

In its boom days, Ravendale had a hotel. A man by the name of Cole owned the hotel, and in the hotel was, of all things—a bar. One evening a group of the local citizenry was gathered there, doin' what people did in an old western bar, drinking, telling stories, and visitin', when along came Joe Frederick. Now, it seemed that Joe had some kind of a bone to pick with Cole, who was standing behind the bar serving drinks. An argument arose and grew to the point that Joe began to put the fear into old Cole. Joe was a pretty little guy, but he was well known for what havoc he could inflict upon a man's body when he lost his temper. Cole, losing his composure and his courage, ran downstairs and locked himself in the basement. At first, it looked like this would end the festivities for the evening, until one enterprising fella' by the name of Lambert Stradt, got behind the bar and set up business for himself. Of course all the drinks were on the house, and before the night was out, every bottle in the place was empty. Now Cole, he took great insult at the way he was treated, and when the party died down, and everyone went home, and he ventured out of the basement to find all his whiskey gone, he was furious. Restitution must be realized, and so a lawsuit was filed. On the day of the trial, Joe and Stradt were in Joe's wagon on their way to Ravendale, and Joe was coaching Stradt on their defense. Stradt was recently from Germany, and didn't as yet have a good command of *American*, or English either, for that matter. So Old Joe, he'd say, "The judge is going to ask how you plead and you're going to say 'Not guilty'. "Now, you got that"?

"Ja, I don't steal no viskey, and I'm kilty".

Then Joe would yell at him, "No, no! It's not guilty, *NOT* guilty. You've got to get it right".

Well, all the way to town they practiced their *elaborate* defense. As usual, the local populace was there for the *shindig*, the judge arrived, and a makeshift courtroom was set up. The court was soon called to order, and the two defendants asked to rise. The judge then unexpectedly asked them "Was that good whiskey you boys stole"?

Before anybody even realized how clever this old judge was, up jumped Old Stradt. "Ja, Ja, goot viskey".

The old judge, he looked the two up and down, watching them squirm for a minute, then down comes the gavel with a bang, "Well, if it was good whiskey, I believe I'd have stole it myself. Case dismissed"!

A frivolous law suit didn't last long in those days.

JUNIPER JIM AND THE DEMISE OF COUNTRY JUSTICE

The case of Juniper Jim was a much more serious situation, and was the beginning of the end for true country justice. Jim, a neighbor of ours, a true blue character, lived on the opposite side of Spanish Springs Mountain from us.

My father was a young man at the time of this incident. At that time, the McKissick Cattle Company was the big ranch on our end of the Plains, running thousands of cattle over many thousands of acres. Most of the other ranchers were small time family ranchers, like ourselves. It was understood that the Mckissicks were generous, and good neighbors, and when some of the poorer folks, like Juniper Jim, got hard up, they could go and *take* a Mckissick steer to keep food on the table, and if they didn't abuse the privilege, nothing would be said. But then the new, younger generation of Mckissicks began to come into control, and they decided that this practice must stop. They seemed to be more concerned about making a buck, than in helping out some of their less fortunate neighbors. So the crackdown began. Juniper Jim, being the colorful character that he was, made no attempt to hide the fact that he took an occasional Mckissick steer for his own use. This *vile rustler* must be now put away.

A formal complaint was made, and a Deputy Sheriff from Susanville came out, incognito, to get the necessary evidence. He came under the guise of a hunter, wanting to know if he could stay with Jim for awhile, and bag some of the local game. And like all of the homes on the Plains, company was always welcome. Jim was no exception.

At that time the table was pretty bare at Jim's—mostly beans. The supposed *hunter* kept asking if it wouldn't be nice to have a little beef on the table, and suggesting that Jim go out and bring in one of them Mckissick steers that were so plentiful round about. Jim, he'd just shrug and say "Go ahead and take one", but Jim wouldn't do it himself. The deputy tried everything he could think of to coerce him into rustling a steer, and when every attempt failed, finally went himself and slaughtered one, blamed it on Jim, and hauled him off to jail.

Now one thing was sure. People stuck together on the Plains when there was a crisis. And if Jim said he was framed, then he *was* framed, and that was taken for the truth. My Grandpa got a bunch of the neighbors together, and they raised money for his bail, hired a big-gun lawyer from Reno, some hundred and fifty miles to the south of us, for his defense. Eventually, he was acquitted, but the cost was dear. Not just in terms of money which was so hard to come by, but this marked the beginning of the end of *true country justice.* People on the Plains just decided they'd be better off not having any formal law, and just stopped inviting lawyers and judges out to our piece of the frontier. And I reckon the lawmen had plenty to do keeping them *civilized* people under control to be worrying about a little bunch of *wild cowboys* out on the Plains.

BLOOD OUT OF A TURNIP

There had been a pretty bad train wreck down in the Honey Lake Valley, and the railroad was auctioning off a lot of twisted steel, junk and a couple of railroad cars. Our friend and neighbor from up on the north end of the Plains, and fellow Basko, Pete Mendiboure bought a railroad car which he wanted to use for building a bridge. A bunch of scrap iron came with the deal, and since he had no use for that, he made deal with some junkie sort of a guy to take the scrap in trade for hauling the railroad car to Pete's place. This slick dude took the scrap iron all right, but then refused to haul the railroad car for Pete.

I don't know where Pete came up with the idea that he could get satisfaction through the *civilized* (in)justice system, but he ended up suing in a court of law—and lost. After court was adjourned, and people were moving out into the hall, this gutsy feller was standing there loudly bragging to some friends about winning the case, and was heard to express the old adage, "You can't get blood out of a turnip!"

Now I mean to tell you Pete was normally a very easy going guy, and good thing too, because he was a big and powerful man. This fancy city feller just managed to push Pete over the line. There may not be any justice in the modern court system, but there *is* blood in the turnip. "I'd have hit him again too", said Pete "if so many guys hadn't jumped on me and held me back".

TRUE JUSTICE MAY NOT BE DEAD (But only in Nevada)

Out in the middle of nowhere Nevada, and if you've ever been through Nevada, you know how just how *nowhere* that can be, one of the Horn brothers from the family who had originally owned the Horn Ranch in our area, was living out his retirement years.

Anyway, Horn, whose first name has disappeared out of my head, was living far from *civilization* along one of the few state highways that run through Nevada. He puttered with mechanics, and welding, and was a kind of Jack-of-all-trades handyman. Consequently he had some various and sundry chunks of metal, car parts, and other miscellaneous such treasures laying around on his place.

This was the time that certain highways were being designated *scenic*, and this highway—hundreds and hundreds of miles of nothing but sagebrush—was suddenly declared scenic. Horn was curtly ordered that he must remove the junk from his property. So Horn, not being a guy to make trouble, arranged with the US of A Forest Service, who owned the land behind his place to move his *treasure trove* out of sight in the back.

But then, as is not uncommon, there was a change of regime and a change of attitude in the Forest Service, and Horn was ordered to move his *junk* off of USFS property. So he did. Moved it back onto his own place, and there it sat.

In no time he was being ordered by the authorities once again to get that unsightly junk away from the gorgeous, beautific, super scenic state highway. He refused, and soon found himself standing before a judge. The judge, being a fairly honest guy, but being obligated to uphold this new law, which was considered by locals, and many others to be a silly infringement of property rights, offered Horn a deal. He said, "I'm going to fine you $100, and 30 days in jail, but if you'll just pay the fine, I'll wave the jail sentence". "No deal". Says Horn. "I'm not moving my stuff again, and I'm not paying any fine".

So, he served his 30 days in jail. He ate 3 good meals a day, while his wife sat at home and lived on his Social Security retirement, and at the end of the 30 days he went back home and resumed life as normal. Except that now when authorities come by beg him to move his junk away from this magnificent marvelous scenic highway, he just smiles and sends them on their way. Seems there's some kind of deal where you can't be convicted of the same crime twice.

How rare is it when the little guy—the nobody—wins against the mighty government? Rare as teeth in a chicken, I'd say.

WHAT ABOUT THE BIG GUY?

I don't want you to get the wrong idea about something. From my writings, it may seem like I don't have respect for The United States. I think you might get this idea also if you were able to talk to any of the pioneers, homesteaders or cowboys. I want to be perfectly clear on this. I and all the others I know from the Plains have a powerful love and respect for America and what She stands for. And what She *stands for* is the Constitution, individual freedoms, governmental checks and balances, individuality, self reliance, independence—in short, the PIONEER SPIRIT.

What I don't respect is meddling power hungry bureaucrats, and powerful wealthy dynasties filled with greed for money and power. Further, I do not respect a *civilization* that is destroying the PIONEER SPIRIT—THE SPIRIT OF AMERICA! Sorry! I just had to interject a little fillyossify here.

11

DAD AND OTHER BROKEN BONES

CAN'T FIND YOUR TOES?

Pioneering, homesteading, and cowboying was a rough business. I reckon it was nothing short of a God-given miracle that any of us survived beyond infancy. My dad was the occasion of more than one such miracle. Actually, quite a few.

Dad was really good with an axe. He could swing an axe from the right or left with precision accuracy. And maybe he was extra good because of something that happened when he was a young man of about twenty years. He and his younger brother Johnny were a couple of miles up the mountain behind the ranch cutting firewood. There was Dad standing astraddle of a juniper log, chopping limbs off of it when the axe hit a limb with a glancing blow that kind of kicked it to the side where it came down right on his foot, removing the two toes right next to the big one. That ended the woodcutting for that day.

Johnny helped him onto the horse they'd brought along, but the motion of the horse made him sick, so Johnny mounted up and galloped down the hill for help. the old crank phone was used to call up Ravendale, and everybody from town, all dozen or so people, rushed to the ranch, and some of the guys came on up the hill and met dad as he had walked about halfway home. He had kept his boot on, and that had kind of held his foot together so he didn't bleed plumb to death, but he said with each step, he could see blood squirt out.

Jim Godman, who had been in the army in the Phillipines and had had some medical training did some preliminary work and probably saved Dad's life. Next he was loaded into somebody's Model T Ford and headed off for Susanville 60 miles away. About half way they were met by Doctor Call from Susanville who then took over the medical treatment. That was the first time Dad had ever seen a doctor and it turned out to be quite a deal. Dr. Call did such a bang-up job of fixing his foot that there was a big write up about it in a medical journal. Dad had a distinctive walk after that, and always had to have his boots custom made since one foot was quite a bit different than the other what with two toes missing.

I SAID SHAKE A LEG—NOT BREAK A LEG

Dad had a lot of mishaps over the years. He wasn't accident prone—he *was* impatien*t* with animals that were a lot bigger than he was—and that spells trouble. The last time Dad broke his leg, I was about ten years old. We had finished wintering our cattle at the Spanish Springs Ranch seven miles south of Ravendale, and were getting ready to drive them home. Smitty and Britches, the two workhorses were there as we had been using them for the feeding, and so they had to be taken home too. Dad had taken Smitty's halter rope and tied it to Britches' tail, and then tied Britches lead rope to a fencepost. The plan was that I would lead them as we drove the cows home. So we mounted up, me on Peanut, Mom on Brownie, and Dad on Chappie, and started to round up the herd. There was some snow on the ground. We started pushing the cows along when suddenly a heifer whirled and started to run back. Chappie instinctively spun around to try to stop her, and slipping on the slick snow, fell flat on her side full on Dad's leg.

Dad kicked loose of the stirrup as she got up, but sure enough, there he lay in the snow with a broken leg.

That changed all our plans for sure. We figured we'd just turn the two work horses loose, and leave them and the cattle there for a few days. But then another dilemma arose. Somehow Smitty had got one of his front feet up and over his own halter rope, and was standing there with his leg tangled in the rope. His massive weight had pulled the short lead rope so tight Mom and I couldn't get it untied from Britches' tail. (I'm gonna interject a little secret here, if you promise not to tell.) I always carry a pocketknife and even though I had got out of school early for the cattle drive, we were forbidden to carry knives at school. So when Mom asked me if I had my knife, she had a rather hopeless tone about her. I hesitated a bit, myself, knowing full well how strict Mom could be with disobedient sons. But as they say, you got to do, what you got to do, so I pulled out my knife and cut Smitty's lead rope. I ended up being the hero. Whew! I carried my knife from then on—Mom's and my little secret.

So anyway, we got some help from a Joe Trumbull who happened to be plowing snow on the state highway nearby. He helped us get Dad loaded into the pickup so Mom could drive him to Susanville to the doctor and Joe drove me on home.

When Dad got to town, the doctor x-rayed his leg. A nurse was called to cut the boot off so they could set the leg and so on. But Dad said there was no way they were going to ruin his custom made nearly-brand-new boots. So Mom and the nurse each took him under a shoulder and held on tight while the doc pulled off the boot, the bones crackling audibly. When they again x-rayed the leg, they discovered that in removing the boot, the bones had set in place and all that was left do was put the cast on and send him home. He was always kind of proud of having saved his boots, and getting his leg set at the same time.

IT'S A LONG WAY DOWN FROM A WINDMILL

Frank Amias, (A fellow Basko and Grandfather's one-time partner—see next chapter) was working on a ranch seven miles to the east of Termo. He was up on a windmill, and somehow managed to fall off. The ground broke his fall—and his back. Like all pioneers, he was used to working alone. No help would be coming by—maybe for days. So Old Frank, he managed to somehow pull himself up into his old Model T Ford, and drove himself into Termo for help. In the end, he survived, but had some residual problems, and in his later years had to have one leg replaced with a wooden one. He'd visit our ranch, when I was a little boy and he'd show me that wooden leg and rap on it with his knuckles. "I bet you can't do that on your leg." He'd say. Frank didn't always win his bets, as you will see elsewhere, but he'd have won that one.

TOUGHER THAN HORSESHOE NAILS

Pete Mendiboure, or Mendiburu if it were from the Viscaino dialect, tanslated means Mountain Head or something like that. And Pete *was* a mountain of a man, and tough as horseshoe nails to boot. The following story is so fantastic I doubt if I could believe it if I didn't know for my self that it is true.

Pete had a ranch at the north end of the Plains, and if it weren't for the fact that he was a fellow Basko, we probably wouldn't have known him very well. Even though the Plains are only about 30 miles long,   north to south, we didn't travel much, and most of our association was with the citizens in the south end where we had our ranch.

Anyway, one day Pete was riding his much beloved mule, Josephine, up around what he called the big reservoir, about 6 miles from his house. Something or other got Josephine stirred up, and she went to bucking and managed to separate herself from her rider.

When Pete came to, he was lying in a pile of lava rocks with a broken wrist, a broken neck, and scalped—well, not quite completely scalped—just that a sharp lava rock or something, had partially disconnected the skin of his forehead from his skull. Still connected over his eyes, there his scalp was hanging down blocking his view. He couldn't see, but I'm sure *you* can see—what a fix he was in.

Pete knew that no help would be coming for many hours, and that if he wanted to survive he had to save himself. He managed to get on his feet, and get back on Josephine, but he couldn't manage her with only one good hand, and his scalp blocking his view. Besides he couldn't keep his head up what with a broken neck.

So, he got back off, made a makeshift splint for his neck by winding his lass rope round and round 'till it sorta held his head up. Then with his one good hand, he held his scalp up to clear his view, and not willing to desert Josephine, he walked and led her all the way home. I think if it'd been me,

44

after what she'd done, I'd have walked off and left the old hay-bag there to starve. But Pete loved his mule.

HOW DID IT END UP

How did it end up that all the broken and wounded stories were about Baskos? Is this some kinda discrimination or something? I don't know, but that's just how it ended up.

Nevertheless, all the pioneers, homesteaders and cowboys were fiercely independent and self reliant. That is what made America the great country it is today. But I fear we seem to have lost that spirit in modern *civilized* America. Now a lot of people want to blame somebody else for their own follies, and sue somebody and so on. How shameful!

12

WHAT THE BLUE BLAZES IS A BASKO?

THEM CRAZY SHEEP-HERDING BASKOS

Basque—Basko. This term for my father's people originally was somewhat like the N word for black people. On the Plains we were referred to as Baskos, coming from the Spanish word Los Vascos (Basques). Over many generations the name has earned at least a small degree of respect. The real name for the people is Euskal Dunak. Basque names are impossible to pronounce—sometimes even for the Basques.

In America, the Basques became known for their ability to herd sheep. Maybe it was not so much their ability to herd sheep as it was their ability to work alone. Most survived the loneliness—some went crazy from it. My great uncle Dick Castneleas came to America and took his first herding job at the age of 14. He told me that many were the nights he cried himself to sleep, all alone out in the mountains.

Because of the sheep herding reputation, we were at times referred to in various derogatory terms, some of which were so vile I can't even print them as a gross description. I'll just leave it to your imagination. The following story, if you choose to read it, may be one of the reasons we were sometimes referred to in such negative terms. This coupled with the fact that cattlemen in general disrespected sheep ranchers or sheepmen as they were also called, led to a lot of bad press for the Baskos.

MAKIN' WETHERS
Gross rated: Skip this if you're squeamish.

One of the messy jobs of a sheepman, or a sheepherder is that of making wethers out of buck lambs. That is the same thing as making a steer out of a bull. In the areas of the country where sheep are run, there are a lot of stories and rumors (mostly untrue) about what the Baskos do to the sheep, one being that they bite the testicles off of the male lambs. There is enough truth in that one to warrant an explanation.

Here was standard procedure for castrating a male lamb, whether you were a Basko, or a *white man*. A helper would hold him for you, and you'd kneel down in front of the lamb, and with your very sharp pocket knife, cut off the end of the sack. Now here is where the process is different from castrating a bull calf. The testicles of the lamb are very small by comparison and to complicate the matter, when you cut off the sack, they suck up inside the lamb where you can't get a-hold of them with your fingers, like you can on the calf. So what you had to do was to use the thumb and forefinger of both hands, and squeeze around the base of the testicles, kind of like trying to pop a giant pimple. By doing this you could get them to stick out a little bit, just enough to get a-hold of them one at a time with your teeth. (In recent times, a pliers-like tool has been invented to replace the use of teeth.) You'd get a good solid bite on it, and to under-exaggerate, the lamb didn't like it. He went to squirming and kicking and bawling and fighting with all his might, while you tugged that little thing out, scraping the sinews back with your knife, and finally severing it altogether. Then you repeated the process on the second one, the blood running down your cheeks, and all over the front of your shirt. For an outsider to watch this, could turn his stomach, but when you grew up with it, it was just part of a day's work. To top it off, you could enjoy a real delicacy by taking those doo-dads, washing them up, breading them, and frying them up, at which time they became known as mountain oysters.

A VENOMOUS SITUATION (Back to G rating now)

Dad told me of one herder he knew many years ago. He was a new herder, fresh from Euskal Herria (Basque Country), but determined to make a new life in America. The herders lived in tents in those days, and had a mule, a supply of food, a sheepdog, and of course the band of sheep. In America they are called bands, not flocks. A band of sheep consisted of somewhere between one and two thousand ewes. Anyway, this herder upon waking one morning, reached under his cot to get his boots as usual, but instead of coming up with a boot, came up with a rattlesnake latched onto his finger. There are no rattlesnakes in Euskal Herria, nevertheless he knew right away, from the intense pain that he was in deep trouble. No help would be coming for a week or more when the camp-tender would bring him a new supply of food, so by his instinct to survive, he went outside the tent, picked up his hand axe, and removed the stricken finger. He survived—less one finger.

PETER JOHN

Peter John was one of the herders who spent too long in the mountains, and drank too much ordoa (wine). Livin' all alone out on the range could surely scramble a herder's gray matter. In truth though, you should have compassion for Peter John. His mental deficiencies probably began long before he was a herder as a result of mistreatment during WWII. He had been in the French army and was captured when the Nazis first invaded France. He spent several years in a Nazi concentration camp. What little food they got was just thrown out on the floor in the middle of thirty or forty men. The only clothing they had was what they wore. They were never given opportunity for a change of clothes, or a bath. For those who survived with any sanity at all, it was nothing short of a miracle.

Pete Mendiboure, employed Peter John for a number of years as a herder, and it was there that I got acquainted with him. Peter John was a really nice fella, but talked kinda funny—partly because he'd had some teeth problems. Eventually he had managed to get to town and get a set of false teeth. He never did get back to town though to get them properly adjusted, and his uppers were way too loose. So when he talked, his words came out at one speed, and his teeth kinda sat there in his mouth and clattered along at another speed. Sometimes as his mouth moved around the words, his lower jaw went up and down, and his upper teeth just sat there tight on his lower teeth. You could get as crazy as Peter John just watching him talk.

He was big on dental hygiene, though!? After he finished a meal, he'd always pull out his teeth and wipe them off on his jeans which hadn't seen hide nor hair of a washing in many months—maybe even in their entire lifetime—and then pop 'em back in his mouth.

FRANK AMIAS

Frank Amias, or Amos as he was called was at a time long before I was born, Grandfather's partner, and a fellow Basko. Frank had a powerful thirst for the whiskey—the cowboy drink of choice. Other than that he was one great guy.

Around the turn of the century, Frank drove their herd of cattle to the railhead in Amadee, down in the Honey Lake Valley. The plan was to sell the herd, and split the money between him and Grandpa. Well, he sold the herd all right, but then went to the local watering hole, got a little whiskey, got in a poker game and lost all the money. After that he was still a Basko, and still a friend, but never again a partner. In 1910 Frank made up for his gambling fiasco by putting up the $100 it took to buy the materials to build our ranch house on the homestead.

FROM IDAO TO IDAHO

Ignacio Urrutia while in the Spanish merchant Marine, came to America at the age of 18. While docked at a port in Delaware, he jumped ship and to hide his real identity changed his last name to Idao, the name of a friend back home. He had an aunt in Boise Idaho who helped him come west to become a sheepherder. He had been raised in a city, and knew nothing about sheep, and had it in mind that he would work in a store, but a Basko is a Basko, and in America a Basko herds sheep. So from his aunt's place he traveled to Emmet, Idaho where he went to work herding sheep for one of Idaho's biggest sheepmen, Andrew Little. (I guess that made him a Little Big Sheepman . . . . I'll let you think on that one for a minute.)

Andrew informed him that here in America, *Idao* was spelled with an H, and so our Basque friend became known thereafter as *Idaho*. And so, Idaho went to work herding sheep. He was driven out into the mountains, and dropped off with a band of sheep, a mule, tent, cot, dog and some food. He was informed that a camptender would be by in a week with fresh supplies. There he was! All alone for the first time in his life with nothing but the western skies and wide open spaces for as far as the eye can see, with a bunch of strange wooly critters bleeting and blatting. At nightfall, the young Idaho bedded down and all seemed well. In the morning, quite a few sheep were still hanging around. By nightfall that night, there were quite a few less. After several days, every last sheep had wandered off to pastures of their own choice. "I thought maybe they didn't like me, or something", Idaho says, recalling those first days.

Well, you can bet that he got some *very specific* instructions about taking care of sheep when the camptender showed up the following week. The sheep were located and gathered from miles around, and once again Idaho was left alone, and thus he remained through the entire summer. He managed to some how, kinda keep the sheep together after that. Strangely, that fall when all the bands of sheep were brought to the home ranch for wintering, Idaho's sheep weighed in better than any of the other bands. In his own words, he "Never knew anything about herding sheep". He did know something about working in a store, though, and ended up owning his own Mom and Pop grocery store in Susanville, where he was much beloved by all.

HOW TO PARK YOUR CAR (OR NOT)

Some years back, my brother Don, his son Gene, and my sister Linda, visited our relatives in the Basque Country. The Basques were not many years free from the deadly oppressive, genocidal rule of the ruthless fascist, Francisco Franco. The Basque people were advancing rapidly, industrially and economically. So the automobile was finally becoming available to the people. One of the family, Josetxu, (Little Jose') had obtained an automobile and my brother being an American, as it was supposed, would be familiar with how to operate one of the things, was encouraged to borrow the car for getting around.

Upon returning from one excursion, Don, in preparing to park the car noticed some faded yellow on the curb, but having been told by the family that it was ok to park anywhere except wherever there was a certain whacha-ma-callit that looked like a barber's pole, he went ahead and wiggled the car into a very small space between two other cars.

The general use of the automobile being still in its infancy, as it would be expected, the laws and rules were not yet uniform. It turned out that the faded yellow paint was there to reserve parking for certain officials during certain hours. So a parking ticket appeared on the car. Don, being accustomed to our American form of regulation figured he'd better take care of the ticket. He discussed the matter with Josetxu's mother, Trini, who being a *character* worthy of note in her own right, adamantly told my brother to ignore the ticket, which of course he planned not to do. So late one evening when Don and Trini were out for a walk, he asked her to show him where City Hall was, thinking that on another day, he would go in quietly take care of the ticket. That way Josetxu wouldn't get in any trouble, and Trini would be none the wiser.

However City Hall was open that time of night, and upon some interrogation by Trini as to why Don wanted to know about City Hall, it was decided to go in right then to take care of the parking mistake. Trini, acting in a manner that wouldn't surprise those who know her, took the ticket to the officer in charge, and immediately lit into him. "What do you think you are doing giving this man a ticket. Don't you know anything? He is our relative visiting here from America. How is he supposed to know what our rules are." . . . and on and on she went 'til she finally ran out of breath.

When she finally paused to come up for air, the very nice public officer quickly interjected, "Well what would he like to do about it? Does he want to pay the fine, or does he want to be forgiven"?

Don, being a pretty practical guy, quickly studied his options and opted for being *forgiven*. The officer then shook his finger at him, and said to him (in English), "No More"!

Don assured him "No more"!

Oh for the times when government was nice to people! I hope the Basques never *progress* to our American level of *civilized* regulation.

13

SCHOOL DAYS

ONE TEACHER, ONE ROOM, ONE SCHOOL

The Ravendale School was built around 1915. The entire school was built with materials donated by the community—right down the the last nail. There was no contribution whatsoever from the government. In the way of government, we had the Post Office, the County Road Shop, and often the interference of the Bureau of Land Management, and that was about it, as far as government services on the Plains was concerned.

In the beginning, the school consisted of 4 walls and a roof. Eventually, a generator shed, kitchen, and two indoor flushable toilet rooms were added.

Dad started school, by staying with relatives in Secret Valley, 20 miles to the south, which had a school before Ravendale. Then the Ravendale School was built, when he was in the third grade, and he attended there after that. It was a 6 mile horseback ride, or wagon ride from our ranch.

For a long time, there were some scattered boards and other left over construction materials laying out behind the school. A brand new school term was beginning with a brand new teacher. The kids were testing out the new teacher and giving her a pretty bad time, and one day when she went down the hill to the Ravendale Hotel for lunch, the kids all got busy with boards and nails from out back, and completely boarded over the windows and doors of the schoolhouse. Then they hid in the brush nearby to see what would happen. When she returned she took one look around the school, turned around, walked back down the hill, packed her bags and caught the next train out of town, never to be heard of again.

The new found kid-power didn't last long. A new teacher was hired—this time, a man—a tough man with experience who put things in order on the very first day. In those days, a teacher had the power to discipline kids with whatever punishment he chose, and this teacher chose corporal—and the parents gave full support. They wanted the school. Most of them had not had any opportunity to attend school, and to them an education for their kids was of utmost importance. If a kid got a spanking at school, there was a good chance he got another one when he got home.

BRING BACK THE OUTHOUSE??!!

Personal duties were still addressed in the outhouses. One for the girls, and one for the boys. There was this kind of rite of passage for the boys. Every boy worth his salt had to at some time, tip over an outhouse. I reckon that was about the worst thing a boy could do. There weren't any drugs, and stuff like that. And any real criminal stuff was out of the question. There were plenty of little mean and ornery things we did, but nothing ever really serious. But you just didn't have any reputation at all if you hadn't tipped over an outhouse.

So anyway, one day the boys at school got up the courage to give it a try. One recess we went out to the boys' outhouse, and all got on one side. All four or five of us—and we all started rocking it back and forth. I think maybe we were all hoping we couldn't actually do it, because it didn't seem like we were trying very hard. I know I would have been fine with forgetting the whole thing, but I wasn't about to say so. So anyway, we rocked and rocked, and finally over it went hitting the ground with a whump and a little cloud of dust, leaving the hole open, gaping up to the sun. Luckily none of us fell in when it went over. I think I was more scared of that maybe happening, then being afraid of the trouble we were going to get in.

No one saw us tip the outhouse over I guess, because back in school nobody said anything. But sooner or later don't you think someone was bound to notice? So it wasn't more than a day or so that Mrs. Gould called all us boys to the front of the class and wanted to know if we knew who tipped over the outhouse. I mean really!? There were only about 5 boys and 5 girls in the whole school. How could she possibly suspect any us boys? (Like as if the girls did it.) Anyway, we all denied any knowledge of it, sticking together just like we had planned, until a few days later when one of the boys got mad at one of the other boys about something, and in revenge, he went and told the teacher that we had done it. So we all got in trouble. I mean, after all, we knew it was coming sooner or later anyway, so we were all a little relieved that it was going to be over now. Funny thing, I don't think any of us got a whippin' over that little deal. We just got a good chewin' out. I reckon everybody knew a boy had to tip over the outhouse. If that was the worst trouble a boy could get in today wouldn't it be wonderful? Maybe we should bring back the outhouse to give boys something better to do than getting into drugs and stuff like that.

PRIDE AND PREJUDICE

Eloise was the only black kid in school. She was a year older than me, and my good friend. She was at our house many times, and sometimes spent the night with my sisters.

Most everybody didn't notice that her skin color was different. However, one day at school, one of the boys called her the *N* word, and man oh man did that stir up a hornets nest! All the kids in the whole school (eight or ten of us) jumped up in defense of Eloise. It was decided, after a bunch of threats this way, and then that way, that the issue would be settled by a fight between the two of them after school. Mrs. Gould, our teacher, of course knew nothing of any of this, so right after school someone checked to see that she was busy at her desk, and the fight began. The punches were flying, Eloise swinging like a windmill, the tears running down her face, but making not even a whimper. And her opponent slugging for all he was worth, and all the rest of us kids gathered round rooting with all our might for Eloise. The fight went on, and on, and on. All the way down from the school, almost to the bottom of the hill. When finally it began to look like Eloise was about to give out, someone sneaked in, stuck his foot out and tripped the adversary to the ground. Eloise landed in the middle of him like a crazed bobcat, all claws and fists, and when she got done with him, he was begging for mercy, and the tears were on the opposite face now. No-one ever called Eloise that word again, you can know that for sure.

BLOOD ON THE SADDLE, BLOOD ALL AROUND AND A GREAT BIG PUDDLE OF BLOOD ON THE GROUND
(Song by Tex Ritter)

I'm remembering a time now at school one day when this one particular boy was giving Mrs. Gould, a real hard time. Now Mrs. Gould was a most patient person, and had a very special way with kids. She rarely had to lay a hand on any of us. But he kept pushing and pushing, 'til finally, he went too far. She grabbed him by the front of his shirt, and slapped him back and forth across the face a couple of times. When she turned him loose, he ran outside, cryin' and holding his face in his hands. After a little while, he came back inside and lo and behold there was blood all over his face. He had this kind of silly look about him, though, and Mrs. Gould wasn't taken aback the least little bit. "Let me have a look at you"! She says, grabbing a-hold of him. Right away, she spotted some marks on his arms. What he'd done, as he quickly admitted, was to take his pocket knife, and scrape on his wrists 'til he drew some blood, and smeared it all over his face. So everyone had a big laugh on the little prankster, and he pretty well behaved himself—just for the rest of the day.

THE WILD BUNCH
The Gilliland family was an unusual lot, even for the Madeline Plains. They were somewhat like you'd expect to see in a comedy movie. They were I guess, what you'd call transients and had moved around a lot, and the kids had fallen behind in school to the point that some of them were too old to be in grade-school. But not having advanced normally through the grades, there they were. They had moved into an old vacant cabin out on Juniper Ridge Road. There were always vacant cabins on the Plains that could be lived in pretty much for the taking. A lot of the area had been homesteaded in 40 acre parcels, and only the toughest survived on

the Plains, and then only on hundreds, if not thousands of acre ranches. So when many of the homesteaders gave up and wandered back off to civilization, they usually left behind a tarpaper shack. Into one such cabin came this family. There were a whole bunch of kids—a very undisciplined bunch to say the least.

One day Walter and Emery, two of the older brothers, got into a fight right there in the schoolroom. Emery, the older of the two started running around the room with Walter chasing him, trying his best to do him great bodily harm. Round and round they went, these two great big overgrown boys, jumping over desks and kids, and Emery laughing and taunting Walter all the way. Finally Walter gave it up and just went outside and took off for parts unknown. It took Mrs. Gould a few minutes to get things back under control. But she did it. She knew how to handle just about anything. We didn't see Walter again for several days. He was like that. He'd take off for parts unknown, and not even his family knew where he went. Maybe he rode a passing freight out of the area. I never did know.

HIGH SCHOOL—SKIP IT

This is just an old cowboy filly-ossify, but when it comes to high school, if I had life to live over, I'd skip it. It ain't worth the punishment for what little education is obtained there. If you happen to be an outsider—a hick from the sticks—a wild cowboy—or if you happen to be undersized, or mis-shapen, different in any way, or if you happen to have gone to a little one room school for eight years, and are now shipped off to the city to live among strangers, you might as well be relegated to the dungeon as to be sent to high school. Well, that's my opinion, and I'm stickin' to it.

OVER THE LOCKERS

I guess I did get something out of high-school. A couple of stories worth telling—and that's about it.

PE was the worst of all. You had to get undressed and take a shower every day. Right there, stark naked in front of all these strange guys—everybody running around bare butt naked, popping one another with towels, and generally running wild. Good gosh! I never saw anything so stupid. People all naked together—wastin' all that water.

My last name starting with G, I seemed to always get a locker between Big Bully G on one side of me, and Less Big Bully G on my right. And there

I was, Little G, not but about half the size of Little Bully G. Every so often Big G and Less Big G would grab me and throw me over the lockers. To my good fortune, there was a pretty good bunch of guys on the other side, and they always caught me before I hit the floor.

THE TRULY SMART ONES GOT OUT

There was this one bully in the metal shop class I was in—a great big Indian kid—at least twice my size. Well, he wasn't so much a bully for picking on littler kids, as he was just plain ornery and picked on everybody. He had messed up some of the kids projects by smashing them with a hammer. And then one day he got the idea that he could heat up a welding rod, and go around poking other kids with it. Now when he came at me with a hot welding rod, it made me really mad, and I picked up a ball-peen hammer, and started swinging. It was like the white man with a war club, and the Indian on the run. I never hit him because I couldn't catch him, and I guess it is a good thing I couldn't.

The teacher finally came out from wherever he usually was, which wasn't in the classroom, to see what the ruckus was. Some of the other kids came to my defense in telling the story, and in the end result was, this big bully got kicked out of school for a while.

Now I had a new problem to worry about. I knew that he knew where I was staying, and I figured he'd lay in wait and beat me to death. But I had spent years working with animals 10 times my size, and had been taught from the beginning to never show fear, no matter how scared I might be. That skill has served me well, many times in life.

Then one day I saw him. He spotted me and came a—runnin'. I puffed up with my best bluff, but inside, I figured I was a goner.

"Hey, Jon"! he says. "you wanna go fishin' with me"? Boy was I surprised. All he had wanted was to get out of school so he could go fishin'. If I'd been as smart as he was, I *would have* got myself kicked out of school, and I *would have* gone fishin'. In all my years of goin' to school, I have never learned how to fish. What a shame!

THE THINGS YOU LEARN IN COLLEGE
(A FANCY FLUSHABLE PRETTY PORCELAIN POTTY)

I know it is hard to believe, but I went to college. I actually graduated from college. The generation of my parents on the Plains never even went to high school, but somehow they got the idea that an education was an important thing to have. I'll venture a guess though, that most of those people were educated in ways that you couldn't get if you went to shcool for a hundred years. I, of course, *had* to go to high school. When it came time for that, I was packed up and shipped off to go board out in the city. I had seen quit a few modern conveniences on trips to various relatives who lived off in civilization, but this living in the city to go to high school was my first real *experience* with such things as electric lights, television, and inside flushable toilets.

So after high school, I decided to go to college. There, I worked for the college maintenance department to earn money for my upkeep and schooling. I did a lot of maintenance in the dorms, and there I got as much education as in the classrooms. We had a phone in the maintenance shop and that's where I learned how to talk on the telephone. When someone need something fixed they ring up the shop, and we'd go take care of it.

One day I got a phone call from the girl's dorm. This nice young lady on the other end says to me "I need you to come up and fix my commode".

I says "Fix yer what"?

"My commode is broken, I need you to come up and fix it".

"Could you please say that a little louder? Yer what is broken?"

"My Commode, My COMMODE. Come right up and fix it!"

So I went to her room and knocked on the door. When she answered, we sorta had a repeat of the phone conversation. Finally, I says to her, "Why don't you just show me where this broken *thing* is?"

"It's right here in the *bathroom*! Where else did you think it would be"?

And of course she led me in to the bathroom. I suppose I shoulda been embarrassed, but at the time I just thought "How stupid! A *commode* ain't nothin' but a fancy flushable porcelain potty. Miss, it's a *toilet*, ok?"

PEE POT
Gross rated description:

I guess it was about this time that I also first heard the term *thunder bucket*. Someone was telling about how in the old days their grandmother kept a *thunder bucket* under her bed. Come to find out, that wasn't nothing but a fancy manufactured pee pot. For us it was a coffee can under the bed, which came in mighty handy on those cold nights when nature called, and it was just tooooo cold to go out to the outhouse.

14

GAMES PEOPLE PLAYED—
NO SISSY GAMES HERE

ROLLER SKATING—IN THE LIVING ROOM?!

There were the usual games like dodge-ball, Annie over, kick the can, hide and seek, and so on. At the ranch, there were a lot of made up games. During the long winters we had some inside games—like roller skating. We had these roller skates that you clamped onto the soles of your shoes, and then skated wildly through the house. They worked great, except once in a while, a skate would pop off, sending you end over teakettle. Every door between rooms in the main part of the house would be opened, and we'd play tag, or just race back and forth through the house. Over the years, we pretty well battered up the baseboards around the house, running into them with the skates. One day after us kids had grown up and gone, someone asked Dad why he didn't replace the baseboards. "Nah! he said. "Those baseboards are memories." Our house was built to live in and boy, did we do a lot of livin' in it.

WATER FIGHTS (And not with little sissy squirt guns)

Our made up games were very physical. In the summer time we had some great water fights. Not just with squirt guns, mind you, but with buckets dumped over people, and throwing one another into the livestock watering troughs and so on. One time after I was married, I and my family were visiting at the ranch. By this time there was electric power, and a real, pressurized water system. I wanted to get a water-fight going so I filled a bucket with water and got up on the roof. Then I sent my oldest daughter, Shawn into the house to get her mother.

"Mom." She says. "Dad wants you to come outside."

"Oh." says she, "What does he want?"

"I don't know, but he's up on the roof with a bucket of water".

I had it in my head that Shawn hadn't seen the bucket, but I was wrong. Next thing I knew, I was under a rain of water from my wife with a hose, and scrambling and clawing, trying to keep myself from falling off the water slick roof. I managed to hang on, but I didn't manage to keep from getting soaked—and laughed at.

FRISBEE FIGHTS?
Gross rated story.

The Frisbee hadn't been invented yet, but we had a better game. It was called cow-pie fights. Maybe this is how the Frisbee got invented. When cows eliminate they leave this mushy thing on the ground that is called a cow-pie. At first it is too mushy to do anything with, but after it dries out, it makes this nice solid disk that can be sailed through the air—at your sister, or brother or some other opponent. Now, if you get a cow-pie at just the right stage of development, it will be nice and crusty on the outside and still green (mushy) on the inside. This was the best weapon ever. If you could hit your enemy with one of these, the outer crust would crumble, and the green stuff would be splattered all over him, dripping down and reeking. And of course, one of your objectives was to NOT let yourself get hit, especially by a half-green cow-pie.

WALK THE PLANK (It couldn't be a simple game of tag)

We called it "Walk the fence". Simply put, it was a game of tag played on top of the corral fences. We had three adjoining corrals, and each interconnected to the barn at some point. In the game, if you were tagged, you were *It*. If you fell off the fence, you were *It*. Some of the fences were made of poles and some were made with sawed boards, which were very narrow to walk on. It was an excellent practice of balance, especially when you were real small, because it seemed like such a long way to the ground. You worked real hard not to fall off the fence. The barn roof was the only *Safe* place where you couldn't be tagged. Little kids spent a lot of time there and sometimes played their own made up games.

Walk The Fence

A CITY DUDE CAN SADDLE A HORSE TOO!?

I never considered riding horses to be much of a fun game. Riding usually meant looking at the north end of a bunch of southbound cows and calves that you were supposed to make go someplace they didn't want to go—Just plain dirty, hard work. However when my cousin, Calvin, from Susanville would visit he often wanted to ride horses. I don't think he ever did figure out just how much fun it wasn't. He loved to get on a horse and gallop around at breakneck speed, playing *Wild West* stuff—I think like something he may have seen on some TV show.

We didn't watch TV, but we knew what the West was. It turns out there was a big difference between the two. One time when I was small I remember visiting cousins in Bakersfield who watched a lot of westerns on TV, and since my dad wore a cowboy hat and boots, they wanted to know if he killed Indians. "What a stupid question". One of my sisters said. "Of course he doesn't kill Indians. Are you nuts"?

But now back to Calvin. There came a time when he thought he was big enough to saddle a horse by himself, and sure enough, he should have been. He was a lot bigger than me, and I was—just barely—big enough to saddle Peanut all by myself. So I showed him how to put the saddle on old Brownie, and how to tie the cinch. Then I told him to walk old Brownie around the corral a couple of times and re-tighten the cinch. He made some comment about how strong he was, and that he had the cinch plenty tight. I said "Well, O.K., if you say so". (For those of you who don't know about such things, when you first tighten the cinch, the horse puffs his chest out against the strain. Then when he relaxes, the cinch is nice and loose, and a lot more comfortable for him. Not a good way to go off playin' *Wild West* games with a loose saddle). Anyway, this is how we rode off that day, me on old Peanut, with my cinch nice and tight, and Calvin on old Brownie *thinkin'* his cinch was nice and tight.

Shortly, we were down in the lower field in the sagebrush, when we jumped a jackrabbit, and the chase was on. All of a sudden, Old Jack took a hard right turn. Calvin jerked Brownie hard to the right. The sudden turn, of course, spun the saddle right around under Brownie's belly, leaving Calvin sailing through the air and coming to earth plowing up the dirt with his nose. He wasn't hurt except for his pride. I almost got hurt tryin' not to laugh my head off. I guess there were a few times when I *did* have fun on a horse.

A Dude Learns How Not To Saddle A Horse

IMAGINATION

I don't quite know how to explain this, but as kids, we were never bored. We had no commercial games or entertainment, but we had imaginations and could always dream up something to do. And whenever kids from the city visited us, they always wanted to play our games. But they didn't want to live there. After a while they were always ready to go back to their electric lights, and indoor, pretty porcelain, flushable toilets.

Over the years, I saw families move out into the country from the city, and invariably, the kids would eventually go wild with boredom. They seemed to have no imagination for entertaining themselves. Maybe this represents one of the differences of being civilized, and being hick from the sticks. I know one thing for sure, I am never bored. *Boring*, maybe, but not bored.

15

MODERN GADGETS AND MACHINES?

A TELEPHONE CASUALTY—ALMOST

I'll never forget our first phone number. Well, it wasn't really a number. It was a ring. Our ring was a long and two shorts. We had what was called, in those days, a farmers line, but we just called it the telephone. It was a battery powered job that had a handle which you cranked in order to ring up a neighbor. Thus also it was known as a crank phone. Not like a crank or prank phone call. These phones were strictly for business, and rarely used for visitin'. Visitin' was meant to be done face to face, eyeball to eyeball, allowing for communication far beyond words.

Each family's ring was different—a series of long rings and short rings. You made a call by cranking the handle in the series of longs and shorts for the family you wanted to reach. Each phone had two bells that jangled when the handle was cranked. When one phone rang, they all rang, so that every one on the line knew who was getting a call, and of course, any number of people could pick up the receiver and listen to the conversation. So when you ended a phone call, you hung up the receiver, and then picked it up again real quick to listen for the clicks of other receivers being hung up, so you'd know how many people had been listening in on your conversation. You could usually tell who was making a call because everybody cranked the handle a little differently. The sound of the ring varied with how hard the handle was cranked, and the longs and shorts varied in length. A primitive caller ID, you might say.

The phone consisted of a wooden box, a mouthpiece, two bells with a clapper in between, a receiver on a cord which hung in a hook, and a crank handle for ringing. That's what you saw on the outside. On the inside were two batteries for providing the "talking" power, and a magneto attached to the cranking handle which provided a higher voltage which jangled the bells on all the phones on the system.

If a person happened to be a bit of a prankster, he could take a magneto out of an old phone, rig some wires to it, get someone to hold the two wires, then crank the handle, and give them a good shock. It wasn't a dangerous shock—just kinda like getting' a-hold of a spark plug on your car. It was great fun to get a bunch of city kids who didn't know anything about magnetos to stand in a circle holding hands, have a couple of 'em hold onto the wires and give 'em all a shock.

That wasn't the only kind of shock you could get off the old crank phone. Whenever there was a lightning storm, the phone would jingle and jangle every time a strike hit anywhere on the line. One time I was standing in the room across from the phone when it took a pretty good lightning strike, and it must have been pretty close. I remember this huge ball of fire coming out of the phone, and coming across the room to where I was, and passing right through me, or around me—I'm not sure what really happened at that point. It didn't hurt me that I know of, but it sure scared the heck out of me. Maybe that's what scrambled my brains and causes me to think the world of civilization is weird.

The crank phone wasn't for kids to use. I didn't learn to use a *real* twist dial telephone until I was in my twenties. I'm still uncomfortable using a telephone. I think the phone is a poor excuse for communicating compared to face to face, beak to beak talkin'—so to speak.

WHAT'S A VACUUM TUBE

You couldn't say we were completely without modern conveniences. We had a battery powered radio. It was a marvel of strange parts—like vacuum tubes, and other fascinating parts. It took two batteries to run the thing, and even though reception was often filled with static noise, and

62

you had to constantly tune the thing to keep it on the station, it was a real joy. And the wonderful thing about it was, not unlike reading a book, you had to use your imagination to conjure up mental images of what you were hearing about. Such things really stick in your mind. I can remember radio programs in detail that I heard years ago—Dragnet, The Lone Ranger, Fibber McGee and Molly, and many others. In contrast I know people who can barely remember the TV show they saw last night. Television is the enemy of imagination.

MUSIC MACHINES

We had a record player too. That preceded the tape recorder, which preceded the cassette player, which preceded the CD player which preceded the ipod, which preceded the ? (Whatever comes next.)

The record player   also called a phonograph, was a spring powered affair. You cranked a handle to wind it up for playing a record. The amplifier, was nothing more than a big metal horn. No electricity was needed to run this thing. It made a scratchy sound along with the music. Modern music without that scratchy sound doesn't seem quite right to me.

Many's the time we would have a family dance in the dining room where the phonograph sat. Mom, Dad, my two sisters, my brother and me. There are quite a few traditions like this from the old days that would be worth reviving.

THE MILKING MACHINE

The most marvelous machine of all was the milking machine. It consisted of two hands—one on the end of each wrist. With all the machines invented by man, none can even come close to matching the marvel of the human hand. That's my unchangeable belief.

There came the time when Dad broke his leg (for the third time), and this is when my milking troubles began. Since Dad couldn't get squatted down on the milking stool with his leg in a cast, and since my sisters had grown up and went off to go to high school, it became my chore to milk old Darlene, the family milk cow. Now if you think working with range cattle is frustrating, just wait till you have to work with a dairy cow. Dairy cattle have been around people enough that they lose a lot of their natural fear of man. And boy can they be cantankerous.

Old Darlene was double cantankerous. She outweighed me twenty or thirty to one, and she knew she had the advantage. After a huge fiasco, I'd finally get a halter on her, and get her tied up. Then came the fight of trying to get the hobbles on her without getting my head kicked off. (Dad could milk her without hobbles as she respected his size and his mature authority.) Me just being a kid and all, she never failed to try to kick me, or kick the milk bucket over, and even with the hobbles on her, she'd often succeed in doing one or both. Then there was her tail to contend with. Always dripping with both kinds of secretions that exude from that end of a cow, she could use that slimy old thing just like a bullwhip to slap you right in the face. So I'd tie her tail into the hobble chains, but no matter how good I'd tie it, she'd keep twitchin' and jerkin' the darn thing 'til it'd come lose, and then *kershplat*, right smack dab in the face again. Well, I'd hang in there 'til I got her milked, one way or another. There were a few times I got so mad I'd give her a heckuva kick. It didn't help the milking go any better, but it gave me some satisfaction. And I ain't too ashamed of it to this day. I'd probably kick her again under similar circumstances.

There were some rewards in the milking though. Sometimes the cats would come around and I'd squirt some milk on them—which they liked, and sometimes my little brother would come around and I'd squirt milk on him—which he didn't like. And then too, there was always fresh milk and cream. Fresh lumpy cream on hot apple pie. Yum-yum!

Hey! Cut That Out!

64

16

THE TROUBLE WITH WATER

WELL, IT'S TIME TO DEEPEN THE WELL

The trouble with water on the high desert Madeline Plains—there was never enough of it. Some families had a well—some didn't. You could get a well by grabbing a pick and shovel and digging a hole in the ground. A rope and bucket worked for lifting the dirt out as you dug. It was nice if you had two people so you didn't have to climb up the ladder each time you loaded a bucket of dirt. Someone at the top could lift it out. (It is really dangerous to dig a well, so don't try this at home). You could usually get a little water at around 40 feet down. In dry years, the well went dry, and you got in and dug it deeper.

When you got your well dug, you covered it over with boards, or concrete, and set up a pitcher pump, or if you had enough money, a windmill to pump the water out. If you raised cattle, you had better have enough money for a windmill. You could buy a windmill in those days through the Sears and Roebuck catalog and have it delivered to your door.

Water was ever on your mind. Livestock require a lot of water. I remember once when our windmill broke, each member of the family took turns standing at the pitcher pump, hour after hour pumping the handle up and down first with one hand and then the other 'til the arms finally gave out, and then another member of the family spelled you off. I think cows take more water than a steam engine.

THE WEEKLY BATH

Bathing was done about once a week whether you needed it or not. People ask me today, "Didn't you people stink awful bad"? But no! it wasn't so. There's something about wholesome hard work that cleans the pores or something. I don't know how it works but people *didn't* stink. Well, most didn't. Believe you me, our *civilized* relatives from the city who wasted a lot of water taking a bath every day, would have let us know if we reeked.

The weekly bath was quite a ritual. The bathtub most commonly used was a galvanized wash tub, barely big enough for an adult to sit in. You put several buckets of cold water in, and then added hot water 'til it was tolerable to get in. Of course, to have hot water meant you had to have a fire in the wood stove. Winter or *summer*! Unless or course you liked an ice cold bath. I don't. Cold water trickling over my body is about as nice as somebody scratchin' their fingernails down a chalkboard. Everybody took a bath in the same water—usually the adults first—and the last one to take a bath came out dirtier than he went in. Or so it was said.

IT AIN'T WORTH THE RISK

For a while, the Smith family were our nearest neighbors 3 miles away on the other side of Morgan Buttes. They had 3 kids, and no well, and had to haul all their water. Those people rarely had a bath. When the kids came to school all red like a lobster, you knew they had had a bath. They said their mom scrubbed them with a wire brush.

Then one day, Wayne, the dad, decided he'd packed enough water and started digging a well. He was down about 40 feet and still hadn't hit water. Then one day the young son Steven was playing out at the well, tossing rabbit pellets down the well to watch them fall, when he slipped over the edge and fell in. This was a real scare. The old farmer line phone began to jangle with the news. Everyone around the south end of the Plains was really upset. Steven was pulled out of the well, and rushed the 60 miles to the nearest doctor, where to everyone's relief, it was found that he had no serious injuries. Wayne went right to work, filled the well back up with dirt, and went back to packing water. "Don't want no dangerous thing like that at *my* place." he said.

17

SEX ON THE RANGE AND OTHER

MIRACLES

G Rated

GOING TO BED WITH A SWEETHEART

At bedtime on unusually cold winter nights, we'd sometimes find a sweetheart to go to bed with—to cuddle up and share warmth. Often times, she wasn't real purty, but she had warmth to share, and that made her real welcome. She came in the form of a flat rubber bottle, called a hot-water-bottle. It had a filling spout in one end. You'd put a kettle of water on the kitchen stove and get it nice and hot and then fill the bottle, and screw the plug into the filler hole. Then off to bed you'd go with your sweetheart. You had to keep moving her around. Maybe you'd put her on your feet 'til they got warm, then you'd move her someplace else. You kept this up 'til the water in the bottle cooled, and by then hopefully you were warm enough to go to sleep.

And *that*, my friends is as sexy as we're gonna get in this book. If I *do* know anything about the sex lives of the folks on the Plains, and surely there was sex—the kids born there prove that—I respect their privacy far too much to share it with you. I hope you ain't too disappointed.

THE LIFE CYCLE

What this chapter is really about is the cycle of the life—the miracle of birth, the miracle of death, and the miracle in between called life.

I'm sure there are those who would consider me to be heartless, and a killer. I killed thousands of Jackrabbits. I killed a few coyotes. I killed other critters that threatened our life or our livelihood. And I have few pangs of conscience about it. But when it came to babies, I couldn't kill anything. If I came upon a den of pup coyotes, there ain't no way I could kill them innocent lookin' little fur balls. Even knowing that they might grow up and cause tons of trouble, I couldn't do 'em in.

I helped bring many critters into this world, even a few human critters, and I helped save the lives of many. I wonder how anyone could look into the innocent pleading eyes of a newborn and not see the desire—"I want my chance to live. Please help me".

I saw many other miracles on the harsh desert Plains. Like the little wild flowers that bloom. On a certain summer day, you might see them. You'd be riding along and on the ground, see a faint tinge of color. Getting off your horse for a closer look, you would see thousands of tiny flowers, not much bigger than the head of pin. There they were, poking their little selves out of the dry hard ground—dry and hard and riddled with cracks. The ground in the Flat would get so dry that it would crack open all over the place, in a pattern like shattered glass. And there those delicate little flowers would be in all their beauty, struggling for their chance at life. By the time the sun reached mid-day, they would be gone, not to be seen again. They left their seeds of life, though, and on another year, if you happened to be out

67

on exactly the right day, you'd see their offspring. There's no end to the miracles of life, if your eye, and your heart is trained to see them.

LAMBING—A TIME FOR CELEBRATING NEW LIFE

We ran a little *bunch* of sheep with about 20 ewes with lambs—not enough to be called a band. In America a flock of sheep is called a band, and consists of a thousand or more ewes. Lambing time was always a thrill. For various reasons, there were always bummer lambs around—motherless lambs either born as twins and their mother not being able to raise both, or lambs whose mothers failed to survive. In addition to our own bummers, Pete Mendiboure, who had a couple of bands of sheep always had more bummers than he could handle and usually gave some of them to us.

At feeding time, these little lambs would come running. They learned real early on, to come when you called. A quart, or fifth size bottle with a rubber nipple, was filled with warm milk, and fed to each lamb a couple of times a day. They'd suck so hard, the milk would froth up and bubble out the sides of their mouths, and they'd butt the bottle from time to time to try to get the milk out even faster. This is something that a lamb, or calf does to it's mother under normal conditions. And all the while, their little tails a-waggling a hundred miles an hour. Your heart got real attached to these adorable little critters.

There was never any problem getting people to feed the bummers. Everybody loved to do it. And if you ended up having to feed by yourself, you could feed three at a time by holding a bottle in each hand, and one between your knees.

CALVING

Calving time was always a real busy season. We always tried to plan it so the babies came in the spring, and most of them did. But cold weather often stays late into spring on the Madeline Plains, and a wet baby hitting the ground on a freezing cold night would die pretty quick if his mama couldn't get him on his feet right away, and get him licked down, and nursed. The cow licks all the birthing material off the calf, kind of like giving it a bath. This also stimulates the blood flow in the baby to help him get going. But often, the weather would be so cold that even with all the effort of the mother to get the baby up, the cold would win out instead. This meant that we had to watch the herd day and night. The cows that looked due to birth soon, would be brought in and kept in the corrals, and barn, and every hour, someone would check on them to be sure a calf wasn't lying on the cold ground, unable to get up.

Sometimes, you'd find a calf on the ground, and all you'd have to do is lift him to his feet, give him a rubdown with a dry gunnysack, and he'd perk right up and be off to look for his momma's teat. (Can I say teat here and keep my G rating? I mean it's ok among us wild cowboy type's, but I don't know about the more *civilized* folks.) At other times, you'd find a calf dead—frozen hard as a board. But it was hard to tell if they were really dead or not. So you checked very carefully for any sign of life and if there was, or maybe even if there wasn't, you'd pick him up and rush him into the house, where you laid him behind the roaring fire in the kitchen stove, and began to rub him down with warm dry gunnysacks. You'd rub and rub, a full body massage, trying to stimulate the blood flow. Then, you'd hold up his chin with your hand, and try to pour a little whiskey down him. If after a while you got no response, you left him lying there, and turned it over to Providence. More often than not, you'd come back in a little while to check on him, and there he'd be trying to get up and go find his momma. On more than one occasion, we had a calf come to life and get up and be wobbling around the kitchen, to our great surprise and delight. Them little critters have a powerful desire to live. Sometimes, though, a baby would die. And though I was exposed to death from the time I can remember, It always caused a twinge of sadness for me when a baby critter died, especially if I'd been trying to save his life.

Feeding The Bummers

THE MIRACLE OF ANIMAL HUSBANDRY

Yep, even as kids, we knew about sex and we were probably as interested in it as kids anywhere, but we also knew the responsibility that went with it. It was life and death serious business about

69

getting the bulls with the cows at the right season so the calves didn't come too early in the spring and freeze to death. It was about helping all newborn livestock critters get safely into this world, and giving them the best chance possible for survival. It was about moving herds from pasture to pasture, from range to range, from water hole to water hole to keep 'em fed and watered. It was about working long hot dry dusty days in the summer putting up hay so the livestock could be fed in the long cold winters. It was about helping with difficult deliveries where the calf or lamb was backward or some other complication. We had to be involved in everything from conception, through gestation, to birth, and then from birth to raising them to maturity. And we knew that the same kind of responsibility went along with being a human parent. Life wasn't going to be just fun and games and a romp in the hay.

MIRACLE OF LIFE—YES VIRGINIA THERE IS A SANTA CLAUS

I once read this marvelous little story about Virginia. If you've never read it, it'd be worth looking up in the library and reading it. And now, I'm here to tell you, Yes Virginia, there is a God. I am certain of it. Oh, I don't know by any scientific testing method. But by the power of the spirit that dwells in all living things, *I know*. And I know there is life beyond this mortality. I've experienced enough of the miracles of birth, death, and the life in between, to know for my own satisfaction. I can't prove it to you—wouldn't even try. But if you'll tune your eyes and your heart into the miracles around you, you can know too if you want to. The sweetest miracles of all are to watch a new little life come into this world, and to connect spirit to spirit with an old timer who has gone on ahead.

18

A LITTLE MISCHIVITY GOES A LONG WAY

GRANDMA'S WINDOW TRAP

When Dad was a boy, he had a bent for mischivity. Like the time when he and his brother and sisters were supposed to be taking a nap. Instead of sleeping, they were wrestling, and jumping on the bed. Grandma kept telling them to settle down and go to sleep, or she would come in and give them a spanking. Finally, she did come in, and Dad, seeing the bedroom window open, made a dive for it to make his escape. In his mad dive through the window, he knocked the stick out that was holding it up, and the window came down on him, pinning him at the waist. Boy, what a perfect spanking pose. Grandma started to whang on him, but with the humor of the situation, she went to laughing so hard she could only stand there and watch him squirm. Fate does sometimes have its own way of serving justice, doesn't it?

FIRECRACKER FUN

One cold wintery evening when I was in my teens, I had a crazy little mischivity urge of my own. Larry Morgan, my very good friend, and his parents and sisters had come to our house for supper, and an evening of visiting. Supper was over, and the grownups were in the living room visiting, and my younger brother and Larry's three younger sisters were at the kitchen table playing some kind of a game. I was a senior in high school, and we finally had school bus service. The bus driver a college kid by the name of Jerry Akey, boarded at our house.

The idea was that Jerry and Larry would boost me up onto the roof of the old ranch house, where I'd to go the living room chimney, and drop a firecracker down into the wood stove below, and shake up the old folks who were visiting there. So they lifted me up where I caught the rain gutter of the back porch and pulled myself on up. I got over the living room chimney, and dropped a firecracker down. I didn't light it, figuring that the fire in the stove would ignite it. It must have landed on the damper or something because it didn't catch. We waited and waited—Larry and Jerry watching through the living room window for all the anticipated excitement. It was dark outside, so no one would notice them prowling around. The firecracker still didn't catch, and by now I was getting a little nervous about what the consequences might be anyway. So it was decided that I would drop a firecracker down the chimney of the kitchen stove instead, and shake up the kids who were sitting around the kitchen table. This time, not to take a chance I lit it with a match.

BANG! The lids of the kitchen stove burst into the air, and the kitchen erupted in a cloud of soot and smoke. As fate would have it, a split instant later the firecracker in the living room stove caught the flame, and

71

exploded. I could hear people screaming and running in every direction in both rooms, falling over chairs and each other.

Now with this moment of confusion, I knew I'd better make my escape. I slithered quickly down the roof to the edge where Larry and Jerry were waiting to help me down. Suddenly the door burst open, and out came my Mom. "What are you boys doing"? She grabbed the broom that hung on the porch. The two accomplices, knowing Mom's methods of discipline, fled like scared Jackrabbits, leaving me hanging from the rain gutter. Mom advanced on me with a fury, and began whanging on me with that broom, but again, thanks to the humor of a situation, and a mother's uncontrolled laughter, I escaped with only a minor beating.

It took a while to convince the other two boys that it was safe to come back and get me off the roof. They knew my mom well enough to know what might be awaiting them. She is very generous, and never reserved discipline to just her own children—and *they knew it.*

The three of us boys spent the rest of the evening cleaning soot out of the kitchen, and repairing the kitchen chimney which had separated at the joints. Even if I'd got a major beating it would have been worth it.

19

JACKASS

MAKE A LITTLE WHATCHA-CALLIT

If the ocean was whiskey and I was a duck, I'd dive to the bottom and drink my way up. (Rye Whiskey)

Moonshine, mountain dew, rot-gut, white lightnin', bootleg, firewater— whatever you want to call it—it was called jackass on the Plains. There was plenty of it made there during Prohibition and since there wasn't much meddling in that area by the law, there wasn't much consequence for runnin' a still.

In spite of that, Old Cap Phelps had some enemies, and got turned in twice, and on the second time spent a little time in the Federal Pen. Before that he had once hired Dad to help him move his still to a location on the Mountain near our ranch where there was a spring. Cap had an old Model A, but it wouldn't go up into the rocky mountains where he wanted to set up. Since Dad had a team and wagon, he was employed to help move the still. It was mid-summer, and Dad was putting up his hay with a crew of hired men. Some of them told him, "You don't want to get involved with that guy. He'll never pay you". Nevertheless, Dad helped him move his equipment. And sure enough, he didn't pay.

After a while, one of the hay crew suggested to Dad, "Since you aren't getting paid, why don't you ask old Cap to drop us off a jug of jackass"? So the next time Dad had a chance to corner Old Cap, he suggested it. That night when Cap drove home they saw him make a stop at the corner of the hayfield, and then go on. Sure enough, he had left a jug of jackass, which immensely pleased the hay crew. Every night for the rest of the hay season there was a jug at the corner. Since Dad didn't drink in those days, I guess the only thing he got out of the deal was a very happy hay crew. Maybe they did a little better job of stacking the hay for him. And then again, maybe not.

MOONSHININ AFTER PROHIBITION

The end of Prohibition didn't end the moonshinin' among the city slickers from down in *civilization*. The first summer I worked at the Dodge Ranch, I wasn't yet in high school. There was however, a couple of young fellers of high school age, from the great *civilized* city of Susanville who were there working for the summer. Jerry and Robin (Petch). It seems that while attending high school in Susanville, they had got all preoccupied with drinking, and since down there in *civilization* they weren't permitted to indulge because of their age, the obsession just grew and grew. So they dreamed up an idea that if they took a chemistry class, maybe they could figure out a way to build a still and make some moonshine. And sure enough, that's just what they did. They rigged up their still outside of town in the forest, and went and bought up all the vanilla extract in town, and started making white lightinin' out of it. Pretty soon, they had a goodly supply, and started taking it to the movie theater on Friday nights, and giving it out to all their friends that came to the movies. So every Friday night the kids at the movies got more and more rowdy, until somebody finally began to suspect something. The cops got to snooping around, and Jerry and Petch got busted. For their probation, they were sent to work for the summer on the Dodge Ranch, way out on the Madeline Plains. What a punishment (joke) that was!!? All they had to do was drive into

Ravendale after work, walk into the bar and buy whatever they wanted for their drinking pleasure.

At that time I had a book that I guess had belonged to my Grandpa which was a recipe book for making alcohol out of just about anything—vegetable or grain. Boy, oh boy! Did they want that book! I finally traded it to them for a really great book of song lyrics. (I figure that if I'd been smarter I could have got a lot more out of them) I still have that book today though, and have had many hours of pleasure from it. I'll make a guess, however that as soon as them two boys turned of age, the fascination of drinkin' probably died off, and the recipe book went in the trash.Ain't that the way it is with some kids. Tell 'em they can't do something, and that's what they will want to do more than anything else in the world. Then when they reach the point where it is ok, or legal, they don't want to do it anymore.

20

THE GREAT WHITE HUNTER SYNDROME

CIVILIZED CITY SLICKERS GET THE SYNDROME REAL BAD

I learned about the syndrome from my Indian Friend, Don Calac. It has to do with the result of putting a gun in the hands of the *white man*. He'll start shooting. He'll shoot anything that moves. He'll then shoot anything that don't move. Then, if he has any bullets left, he'll shoot at nothin'. In the City they even go around shootin' each other. It's a pretty bad sickness. I had a touch of it myself for a while, though I never shot nobody. Most of the old timers on the Plains never had the syndrome at all. But maybe us mountain people aren't really *white*. If bein' *civilized* and bein' *white* are synonymous, I think I'll just claim to be a Basko, and denounce bein' *white*—or *civilized*.

The Madeline Plains is in the heart of prime deer hunting territory, and the mule deer thrive in the high desert. Deer season came to our area in 1958 when the government opened the area up for legalized hunting. The Fish and Game must have advertised far and wide that Mt. Observation and Spanish springs Mt. were now open to hunting because the flatlanders flocked to the mountains in droves—throwing gates open, letting livestock out of fields, dumping trash and beer cans all over the place—and shooting holes in everything. Some hunters even walked into our house in the middle of the night preparing to bunk down—didn't knock or anything—just walked in like they owned the place. Well, we never shot anybody over such things, but we often wondered how the flatlanders would have treated us if we'd come down to the city, set up a tent in their front yard, and left trash all over the place.

HUNTIN' OR GAMBLIN'?

Some years after the area opened to hunting, I was talkin' one day with this guy that owned a gas station down in the Honey Lake Valley. It was during deer season, and he was telling me that one morning just after he opened up his business, a car pulled into the self serve pump. He said he couldn't help but notice that there was a lot of loud talk and hand waving going on among the three men who had gotten out of the car and were standing there with the trunk opened. He figgered he better go out and see what the commotion was all about, so he went and asked if there was something he could do to help them.

"No way", says one of the guys. "There ain't nobody can help us. We came up from the Bay Area (Or somewhere. I forget just where.) to go on a deer hunting trip. Instead we've spent the week in Reno, and now are on our way back home. We just now opened the trunk and realized we left all our hunting gear on the front lawn at home, and there ain't no way we can go home and explain this to our wives.

THEM PESKY JACKRABBITS

In March of 1952 we had an unusually big snowstorm for that time of year. We figgered at least 5 feet came, and when it got done drifting in the wind there were some drifts 15 or 20 feet deep. Then the jackrabbits came. Millions of 'em. It was far enough into what should have been early spring, that they had started their spring breeding frenzy, and now there were rabbits everywhere. Honestly! Many, many thousands of them. And the only thing for them to eat was the hay meant for the cows. Everything was covered under mountains of snow. So all over the Plains, they converged on the haystacks like malignant armies, devouring hay and leaving the cattle to starve. They would stand up on their hind legs, reaching as high as they could, undermining the stacks until the sides would slip down, and then they'd start in again. On some of the ranches where they had remote stacks that they couldn't get to right away, the jackrabbits literally devoured the stacks to the very last straw. And they came after our forlorn little hay stack, which was showing that it would not last long enough to feed the cattle, let alone the rabbits. I learned to kill jackrabbits. Each morning, we'd go out to feed the cattle, pull the team and wagon alongside the haystack, and then Dad with the .22 rifle, and my sisters and I with sticks and clubs would go to killing rabbits.

Goss rated description:

Whack, whack, whack, bang, bang, bang. After awhile Dad would get up on the stack and start pitching hay into the wagon, while us kids continued with the deadly work. Whack, whack, whack, and if you hit a rabbit and didn't kill it outright, it would cry out in the most terrifying scream, kinda' like a baby screechin' when you stick him with the safety pin. Made you whack real hard and fast then, to finish the job and shut that critter up. Day after day. Purty ugly work to say the least.

G rating continued

Even with all our efforts, the haystack disappeared faster than the rabbits, and first thing you know, we were out of hay and had to arrange to move our cattle to another ranch where we bought some hay.

This was the beginning of my getting infected with the Great White Hunter Syndrome. As I grew older I learned to make sport of killing Jackrabbits. I can't say if that's good or bad, but eventually I got over it. The Great White Hunter syndrome, that is.

A DUDE WANTS TO GET THE SYNDROME

When I was15 I bought an old 1935 Chevy pickup. I didn't need a drivers' license on the Plains and had been driving for several years already by this time. That old Chevy was the best rabbit hunting rig ever. It had big front fenders with a headlight on each one. A guy could sit on the fender wrap his legs around the headlight to hang on, leaving both hands free for shooting,

I was in high school at the time and this one city kid by the name of Mike Bennet kept bugging me to take him out to the ranch to go rabbit hunting, so finally one time I did. We took off in the old '35 Chevy, heading down to the Madeline Ranch which was 3 miles to the East of our ranch. When we were coming back, Mike decided he'd like to sit on the spare tire that sat in a tire well just in the back part of the right front fender. This worked really good for a while, and was a softer seat than on the fender itself. There we were clipping down the dirt road (all the roads were either dirt roads or graveled roads) when all of a sudden I notice the spare tire rolling along side, down the road. Then I saw Mike rolling alongside—and Mike's shotgun bouncing down the road. It seems the nut holding the tire had fell off, and there they went—tire, Mike and gun. Fortunately other than a few scuffs on Mike and the shotgun, there were no serious injuries.

Well, maybe it ain't so. I heard a few years back that good ol' Mike had died. I hope it didn't have anything to do with Jackrabbit hunting. Mike was really a good guy, and I don't think he ever did get the Great White Hunter Syndrome.

The Great White Hunter

BEGINNING OF THE END OF MY AFFLICTION

I started working summers on the Dodge Ranch when I was 12. I was mowing alfalfa. The Dodge Ranch had access to a little water, and they tried to raise alfalfa. With the short growing season on the Plains, you might—I repeat, *might*, get one good cutting of alfalfa. Compare that to 7 cuttings in the Sacramento Valley.

One day I was mowing away with the swather (a big mowing machine especially built for alfalfa), and I kept jumping this little fawn. He'd bed down in the tall alfalfa, and I couldn't see him, but every time I'd get close he'd jump up and run a little way and lay down again. Not wanting to cut him up, I'd stop the machine, get off and try to follow him and catch him, but no matter how silently I'd sneak up on him, and how suddenly I'd pounce, he was always too fast for me. Sadly to say, I finally did hit him with the swather, cutting off three of his legs, and then I had to kill him, leaving me with a very haunting memory—those great big brown eyes looking up at me saying "I want my chance to live". I think that was the beginning of my cure from the Great White Hunter Syndrome.

21

KIDS (of the hyouman kind)

SALT AIN'T JUST FOR CURIN' PORK

Kids are the most wonderful of all little critters. I oughta know. I've dealt with all kinds of critters, and a lot of kid critters. I have 6 of 'em myself. Kids that is. And many grand-kids.

Right now, I'm thinking of one my kids. Years ago when my second daughter, Trini, was the youngest, probably around three or four years old, we took a trip to Salt Lake City. I have always been fascinated by all things in nature, and the salt flats, and the Salt Lake really captivated me. When, we were driving along the Great Salt Lake, we stopped to let Trini and her older siblings run and play and burn off some of that wild childish energy that builds up after long hours of sitting in a car. We let them take off their shoes, and wade in the water as it was a nice warm day, and I wanted them to experience the Salt Lake. They were playin' around and splashing as kids would do when I got this idea. I told the kids to stick a finger in the water, and then touch it to their tongue. They did, and then I says to them, "What do you taste"?

The two older kids didn't say anything, but Trini, thought deeply for a little bit, and then suddenly her eyes widened. Recognition came across her face, and she blurted out "Pepper"!

DON'T MESS WITH SANTA'S REINDEER

When the kids were still little, we had a tradition on Christmas Eve, where me and the kids would all climb into my old pickup, and go driving around to see if we could spot Santa making his rounds. The kid's mother always had a convenient excuse not to go along, and naturally, Santa always stopped by our house while the rest of us were out looking for him. Thus it was on one Wintry Christmas Eve, me and the kids (there were four of them at that time.) were all bundled up, and loaded into the old pickup, and off we went in a frenzy of anticipation. It was snowing some, and windy and really a white Christmas, perfect for Santa and his 8 tiny reindeer and sleigh. We drove along for a while, and several times we were pretty sure we got a glimpse of something in the sky. Then suddenly, bounding from the side of the road, right in front of us was a little bunch of deer. Mule deer mind you, and not flying either. The road was snowy and icy, and I dared not slam on the brakes for fear of going into a skid, and sure enough, as fate would have it, I hit one of them—just a glancing blow, but four little kids were absolutely certain I had killed one of Santa's reindeer. I got the pickup to a stop, and got out, to find that the deer was gone—apparently no serious injury. But try to convince four little kids that I hadn't hit Santa's reindeer. I was the bad guy that night for sure, especially for Tonya, the youngest . . . When we got home, Santa had been there, and I was off the hook. Well, sorta off the hook. I'm not sure I'll ever be totally forgiven for that incident.

HOW TO RAISE KIDS (OR NOT)

My brother Don and a neighbor called Shorty Crabtree were working one day out in the Painter Flat area, just over the line in Nevada, where Shorty had leased some land and was running his herd of cattle there. They happened in at the place of one of the local ranchers around noon time. It was traditional that if you came into somebody's camp, or ranch around mealtime, you were expected to come in for a meal and some visitin'. And these folks were traditional enough—in that way at least. So Shorty and Don were invited in. There was a mom and a dad, and several kids running around, one of which was a toddler. When the table was set and the food laid out they all sat down to eat. They were sitting there eating and visitin' when the little one who was in a high chair, got to squirming around and squirmed right out and would have fell to the floor except for the fact that his hind foot (that's cowboy talk for a regular foot) got caught in some part of the chair, and there he was hanging upside down, a-bawlin' and a-kickin'. Well, the dad, he just goes on eating. The mom, she just goes on eating. The baby just hangs there. Don, he was feeling real edgy to do something or say something, but being little older than a kid himself, didn't have the nerve to say anything. Finally, Shorty, himself being old enough and tough enough for most any situation if need be, finally figures he oughta say somethin' to the parents. "Aren't you gonna do something about that kid hangin' there"?

Without missing a bite, the mom snorts, "Hey, it's a tough world. Kids gotta learn to figure things out for themselves".

And that's just what he did. The little guy finally got himself kicked free and fell down to the floor, and crawled off to some new adventure.

It *is* a tough world in the high desert, and people who lived there had to be tough. These people came from a family who had a reputation even among the hardy local citizens for being unusually rough and unsavory. I think they fully lived up to their reputation. And maybe more.

Well, who's to say what parenting method works best for raising kids, and what makes for good parenting. You'd probably say these were pretty lousy parents, but that kid probably grew up to be independent, and made out better in this world than I did. I have never been very successful at adjusting to living in *civilization*, even though my own parents were pioneer tough in their own right. (Not near as tough, mind you as the people I just told about.) *Civilization* is a lot tougher than I am. I barely survived it to tell the story.

22

TELL A STORY IN SONG

FILLYOSSIFY OF BARNYARD MUSIC

You can't talk about the lives of the pioneers, cowboys, and homesteaders without sayin' something about home-made, old-timey, country music—and what a nice way to start winding down the day (Or a book of stories) than with a good old fashioned hoe-down.

I call it Barnyard Music. It used to be called Country Music, but *Country Music* of the modern civilized world had no resemblance to what the country

80

folk used to play in their homes. So I had to come up with a new name for what we did—thus, Barnyard Music.

Music was as big a part of our entertainment as telling stories. It was home-made. It was simple, like the country folk who played it. And they *played* it—they didn't *work* it. Work is what we did every day—hard physical work. Work that left your hands stiff and calloused—not ideal for playing refined high falutin' note-perfect music. Barnyard music isn't about musical perfection—it is all about having fun. I got a very important part of my music theory from an old Indian. You can read about that in chapter 9—Indians.

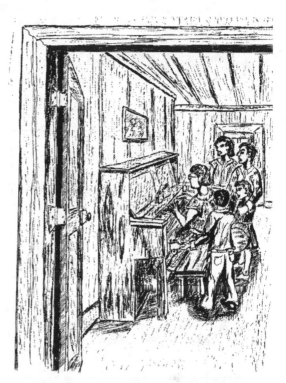

Come On In—Let's Tell A Story And Make A Little Music

My Mom has a special gift—or curse—depending on how you look at it. She suffers from ear worms. That's when you have songs runnin' around in your head and can't shut them off. All day long, at the ranch, Mom would go about her work, singin' and whistlin'. She's got a ton of songs in her head and in her heart.

I have the most pleasant memories of her playin' the piano and singin' after the rest of the family had gone to bed for the night. I slept upstairs, and just the memory of those sounds filtering up through the floorboards soothes my soul to this day.

Whenever company came there was always the visitin' and story tellin'— and there was also good ol' home made music and singin'.

SINGIN' IN THE COLD

We had a very old battered and beaten pickup. There were very few cars on the Plains. Some of my neighbors never owned an automobile of any kind. Pickups were needed much more on the ranches than a car. So it was, that we were able to travel some in a pickup. As kids, we almost never rode in the front. There wasn't enough room. Imagine riding in the back of a pickup when the temperature is below zero, and the wind is blowing snow down the back of your neck. We would bundle up as best we could and wrapped in blankets, huddle as close to the cab as possible to cut some of the wind. Then, we would sing at the top of our lungs. Preferably long songs. Repetitive songs that went on and on. Like 99 Bottles of beer on the wall, There was an old woman who swallowed a fly, My Gal's a corker, etc. Singing with all your might seemed to help increase the circulation a little. Simply put, it was sing loud or freeze.

I PLAY A MEAN FIDDLE (Find the humor in this if you can)

Back in the seventies, I was playing guitar and base in a little country band. Bob Seeley, the leader of the band had been playing locally for many years. Much more than a just a fiddler, he knew how to put a group together, and put on a dance. He could play all night long and never play the same song twice. He had a loyal following, and never a shortage of opportunities to play.

We were playing a regular monthly dance for the Senior Citizens group in Susanville. For a while, my sister-in-law, Alice played piano in the group, and my brother Don, would come along, and call a square dance or two to give a little change of pace.

Then one day Bob decided to move up into Oregon to be closer to some of his family. That sure left a big gaping hole in the hearts of a whole bunch of people. My brother and I not wanting to let the square dancing die out, decided to go it on our own. I picked up a cheap old broken down fiddle, and learned a few hoe-downs and we went to playing square dances around the area. Alice played backup on the piano, Don called, and I played some rough but very fast hoe-downs.

We began to get a reputation, and a little following—up until Don and Alice moved off to Arizona, and I moved off to the Napa Valley, in California. Anyway, one time we got invited to do a square dance at the Mormon Church in Susanville. There was a wonderful crowd there. There were people of all ages, and Don having a wonderful talent for getting people out onto the dance floor, soon had everyone tappin,' clappin,' and dancin' their shoes off. One old boy, appearing to be quite along in years was having an exceptionally good time. I reckon our playin' the old time music and dances brought back memories for him. We did this one called the Virginia Reel, and as was traditional in our part of the country, played faster and faster toward the end. By then, everyone was pretty winded, so it seemed a good time to take a break. So everyone went and sat down on chairs all around the hall, and the old boy, he went and sat down, leaned back in his chair against the wall—and died!!! Stone cold dead! Right there on the spot! Never drew another breath! Massive heart attack! End of story! End of dance!

The next day we looked up the family of this old fella, and went and tried to apologize, but they would have no such thing—said they hadn't seen him have such a good time for years. He had a history of a bad heart, and they all knew the risks. They were just glad he got to check out having such a good time—and with a smile on his face.

Thank goodness, Bob Seeley finally moved back, and I went back to playin' guitar mostly

Many years have gone by now, and I feel free to enjoy telling this story. I tell people, "My fiddlin' ain't really that good, but it *is* deadly." (Remember what I said about Dad teaching me to look back and find the humor in a situation?) Well I laugh about this story now, but I'll tell you what, though! It was no laughing matter at the time.

WOUNDED BY A HARMONICA?

Before the dancehall was built at Termo, the dance location on the Plains was anybody's living room. Somebody'd decide to have a dance and invite the neighbors. Somebody would ride over to the south side of Spanish Springs Mt. and invite Juniper Jim. He cut a lot of juniper trees for fence posts, and that's how he came by the name. Jim played the harmonica, so he was often requested at a dance. As long as anyone was still upright and wanted to dance he would play. If people danced all night long, he would play all night long. By morning, blood would be running down the corners of his mouth from blowin' that harmonica. But stop playing while someone still wanted to dance? No way! Not Jim.

AN OLD TRADITION WRECKED BY *CIVILIZED* FOLK

The country dance changed very little after the dancehall was built at Termo. There was just room for more people. It was still a family affair, and babies would be put to bed on blankets under the benches that lined the hall. There was a little bandstand on one side, and a band was actually hired to come and play. The band could easily be encouraged to play on longer by passing the hat to pick up a few extra bucks. The watering hole (bar) adjoined the hall, and the dancers could easily loosen up the stiff knee joints.

In the old tradition, it was not only proper, but expected that a man would dance one dance with each neighbor's wife sometime during the night. It was a matter of showing respect for your neighbor. There was a lot of proper eta-kit among the people, and things didn't get out of line. The people knew how to control their drinkin', and they knew how to behave themselves. That's the way it was among us un-*civilized* wild cowboys.

But nothing stays the same forever. People began to come from miles around. Since we were far beyond the reaches of the law it was easy enough for anyone to get a little whiskey and age wasn't an issue. This of course attracted people from the *civilized* world. They figured out they could come to the Termo dances and get wild. And so they did—which was finally the downfall of the dances, because them *civilized* folks got too wild, and the dances turned into as much of a brawl as a dance. It seems that *civilized* guys couldn't have a drink or two without starting to get fresh with somebody else's wife or girl friend. Maybe livin' in *civilization* changes the way people treat each other.

FINALLY—EPILOG

Thanks a lot for joinin' me here in the living room. This wasn't quite 1001 Arabian Nights, or 1001cowboy nights either, but we *have* spent a lot of time together. I don't know how many stories I've told. I gotta tell you though, I never get tired of tellin' stories, but I do get tired. And I'm tired now, so I quit—tellin' stories that is. It sure has been a wonderful visit. But the fire here in the living room is about out, and it's startin' to get chilly. And the working day starts at daylight, so I reckon we better be thinkin' about hittin' the hay. You come back real soon, now, and next time you can share your stories. I know you have some.

I hope that you have gained a greater understanding and appreciation for the pioneers and homesteaders, and cowboys that settled the Great American West. They were just ordinary people, but their way of life was so different, and the customs and ways are, I fear, gone forever. If I could, I'd bring back the good things and leave all the bad behind. If I have enriched your life just a little, then maybe I have managed to preserve the good just a little bit anyway. That is my hope.

WHERE DID EVERYBODY GO?

Most of Dad's generation are dead and gone. And what became of all the characters that I grew up with? Well, everybody wandered off and made their way into *civilization*. The women became wives, raised kids, and now have grandkids. The guys went off and did things like driving truck, working here and there. Some run little businesses. They too, married and raised families. I know of only one that stayed on the Plains—my good friend Larry Morgan. He must have had more of the pioneer independence than all the rest of us. It's a tough place to make it—and got harder as the years went by. I don't know of anyone that became famous, although my brother might someday. He is an Interpreter for the National Park Service, and does serious historical research, and is a true historian dedicated to digging out the truth of the past. He is in the process of publishing a 3 volume work on de Anza, who established San Francisco.

I don't know how many of my contemporaries feel as I do. I am caught between two worlds. I can't quite leave the past behind, and I don't quite fit into *civilization*. I am minimally successful by modern standards, but growing up on the Plains taught me to live on nothin' and be happy about it. I know how to enjoy life without all the *consumerism*, and *things* thought to be necessary for happiness by *civilized* folks. So if you were to measure success by happiness, contentment, peace of mind, and love of family, then maybe I've done ok.

Most of my acquaintances think I am "a little odd." And I reckon they are right for sure. I don't think they even believe some of the things I tell them. Most people can't imagine a place in California where some one my age could grow up in the genuine Old West. A place where the winters can get 30 degrees below zero at night, and not go above the freezing point even in the daytime for a month at a time. A place where there was no electricity, and hardly any modern conveniences. I had the good fortune, (or the misfortune, depending on how you look at it) of living in a society of true pioneers, homesteaders and cowboys. Sometimes I ask myself, "Did we really live like that?" I know that we did, but sometimes, it seems like just a dream—the world has changed so much, and the worst of all is that people have changed so much.

The Old Timers were self reliant and independent. They took care of their own needs. At times when that plan came up short, neighbors helped each other. The pioneers, unlike modern *civilized* people needed each other. It seems to me that America has become a people who rely on lawyers, cops, firemen, insurance programs, the government, and so on for nearly everything. I've noticed most people don't even know their neighbors, much less befriend them. I find myself wondering, what ever happened to the Pioneer Spirit of America? It makes me a little sad to think that maybe that Spirit is disappearing.

PROGRESS: WHAT IS IT, ANYWAY?

You can't stop progress. That's what we heard time after time as we watched little bits and pieces of our way of life chiseled away by the modern world creeping in. I don't think it would be so difficult if I could actually believe that *progress* is a direct line forward to things that are better. But I have this nagging fear that what we think of as progress, may really be a large circle in which we just go round and round with things only seemingly improving for certain people in power and that things of an eternal nature never really change at all. In any real sense, maybe the important things only improve when people themselves act better toward each other. To me, that is true progress.

For us, over time, the horse and buggy gave way to the automobile. Taxes kept rising to pay for services that we neither asked for, and in most cases never had. Money became more and more a necessity. Kerosine lamps gave way to the electric light bulb. The horse and plow gave way to the tractor. We watched a steady peaceful tranquility giving in to the race of the rats. (Rat race: I wonder who named it that). Sure enough, we used to get on a horse, and ride all day moving some cattle, and maybe cover a whole ten or twelve miles, and now you can hop on a jet and go half way around the world in the same amount of time. On and on goes progress, until nothing is left but the memories.

The railroad gave way to buses and airplanes. Bus service declined to a deplorable state as the airline industry grew. Now the airlines seem to be dying. What is next? Is your job about to be outsourced? And I think "*You can't stop progress*". And sometimes I think of saying that to some unfortunate friend who has been squeezed out of his job or home. And I could gloat. But I don't feel that way. I just feel sad as I remember *progress steam-rolling* over us. We no longer have our way of life. And we no longer have our ranch. Still, we survived. And you will too. The question is, do you fight this thing called *progress* to try to save your way of life, or is your destruction inevitable? For us, we were few. We had no chance against the mighty powers that be. We should have probably given up sooner. Once you know you are defeated, you can pick up the pieces and move on. Still, I can't help but think of those of you whose jobs are being threatened. There are so many forces at play. Technology changes; social changes; industrial changes; worst of all, changes in government and corporate policy brought on by greed for power and money. My hope for you is that your numbers are large enough that you can combat this dreadful government and corporate policy of outsourcing jobs. It looks like the same kind of *progress* that destroyed the last of the pioneers on the Madeline Plains.

Still, not all is gloom and doom. I believe in a power of God and of good, and that that power will ultimately prevail. In the meantime, if we can just learn to make the best of whatever life hands us life will be good. Life is good if we make it good. It is bad if we make it bad. Every morning when I get up I say "I can smile and make this a good day". Or I can frown and be miserable. The choice mostly is mine. And usually, my days are good.

Well, enough fillyosofising for now. Thanks for reading my book. It's been real nice getting acquainted with you. May you make every day to be the very best that it can possibly be.

GLOSSARY

The following are *daffynitions* of words used in this book (or not). They are listed as they relate to each other—not alphabetically. Some are typical of western lingo—Some are not. Some are invented by the author.

DAFFYNITION. Definition with a little humor or sarcasm added.

AMERICAN. Language used by natives of the Madeline Plains; Sometimes resembles the English Language.

MADELINE PLAINS. Large high desert salt flat, high in the Warner Mountains, covered with sagebrush, coyotes and Jackrabbits; Located in remote area of north-east California; Also called the **PLAINS;**. Also called **THE FLAT.**

FLATLANDER. Anyone not from the Madeline Plains; The only way to get to the Plains is to go up (into the mountains); Everyone else lived in the **flatlands** below; A term meant to be a mild sarcasm.

CIVILIZATION. Place where people lock their doors, have a lot of cops, lawyers, and jails; Place where people don't know the name of their neighbor, and generally treat each other really bad.

HOMESTEAD. A piece of land, 640 acres (or less) which the government gave you if you did certain things, on which land you could torture yourself for the rest of your life trying to scratch a living out of it; Grandpa was a **HOMESTEADER;** Dad was a **HOMESTEADER;** I was not a homesteader, but I lived among the homesteaders.

OLD TIMER. Someone who lived on the Madeline Plains before you did; Or the oldest generation still living; I guess I'm an old timer now.

CHARACTER. Eccentric person; Everyone on the Madeline Plains was a character of some sort. (Except myself, of course) (*My wife disagrees*).

OLD. Term used in front of a person's name, or an animal's name to designate that person, or animal as a character. i.e. Old Tom; Old Peanut, etc.; Has nothing to do with age of person or animal.

OLD PEANUT. (Peanut) My **crazy as a bedbug** mustang horse

DUDE. (Sissy); Drugstore cowboy which was a guy from the city who wore fancy western duds, tucked his pants into his fancy boots, and never, ever, in his whole life stepped in a **cowpie;** Word used to insult somebody; Used carelessly, could get you a black eye;

COWPIE. What the cow drops on the ground when she does a number two; **Green cowpie**—fresh and mushy; **Dry cowpie**—hard and crusty.

COW *STUFF*. Nice word for a not so nice word which means cow manure.

BULL *STUFF*. Nice word for not so nice word, meaning a *big fat lie.*

BUCKAROO. Cowboy; From Spanish word, *Vaquero*, meaning cowboy

COWBOY. Bowlegged guy who spent his life in the saddle day in and day out, seven days a week, for $1 a day, and room and board; Probably a bit crude, smoked **roll-yer-owns** or chewed Days Work tobacco, and drank too much on occasions; Probably never married; Probably took a bath once a month or so; Probably changed clothes now and then; Probably took a few days off work a couple times a year, went to town and spent all his money.

ROLL-YER-OWN. Hand made cigarette; The cowboy took great pride in being able to do this with one handed while he managed his horse with the other hand.

RIDE. What the cowboy did for a living—ride horses and work cattle.

HANKERIN'. Cowboy talk for desire.

BOWLEGGED. What a cowboy gets for spending so much time in the saddle.

SADDLE. Apparatmus fastened on the back of a horse for a cowboy to sit in, and make him bow-legged and butt-sore.

SADDLE HORN. Gadget on the front of a saddle for taking your **dallies**; Item for a dude to hang onto, especially if the horse bucked; A real cowboy would rather get bucked off into a pile of lava rocks and sagebrush than be labeled a dude or sissy for hanging onto the saddle horn—it was just one of them unwritten laws of the land.

DALLIES. Turns of your end of the **lass rope (lasso, riata, etc.)** around the saddle horn to secure it; Hopefully the noose end is around some part of the cow; Good place to get a thumb of finger pinched off by getting it caught in the **dallies**.

RANCHER. Landowner who worked 7 days a week, ran cattle, and had payday once a year or so; **Big rancher** owned lots of land and hired professional cowboys; **Little rancher** owned a little land, and had a wife and kids to help him run his cattle; Always independent and bull-headed; Earned very little money; Probably had some of the less desirable qualities of the Cowboy, but kept them in check (most of the time).

SHEEPMAN. Same as a rancher except he ran sheep instead of cattle; Not highly respected by most Ranchers and Cowboys. Quite often, a **Basko**.

SHEEPHERDER. Basko who tended the sheep while they were out on the range; Spent endless months without seeing another human being; Saved his money (hopefully), bought land and became a **Rancher** or a **Sheepman;** Went **crazy as a bedbug** if he spent too many years out on the range herding sheep.

SHEPHERD. Word found in Christmas carols; Word otherwise never used on the Madeline Plains.

BASKO. From the Spanish word **Vasco**, more commonly known by the French word, **Basque**; Sometimes used as a racial slur; Strange talkin' foreigner who came to America to herd sheep, and earn enough money to buy land; Grandpa was a Basko; Dad was a Basko; I guess that makes me a Basko.

INDIAN. Someone almost never, ever shot by a cowboy; Someone thought of by Hollywood people as always being shot by cowboys.

COWHORSE. What was rode by the cowboy—sometimes; Othertimes the horse dislodged him; (Bucked him off).

BUCK. (1) What a horse does to try to keep you from sitting in the saddle and getting bow-legged and butt-sore; (2) Male sheep—Ram was a word used by dudes; (3) Male deer—Stag was a word used by dudes.

STUD. Male horse with his **doo-dads** left on so he can breed the female horses; Called a stallion by **dudes**.

GELDING. Male horse with his **doo-dads** removed so he can't breed the female horses.

STEER. Bull or bull calf with his **doo-dads** removed.

WETHER. Male sheep with his **doo-dads** removed.

MOUNTAIN OYSTERS. A very delectable delicacy made by breading and frying **doo-dads**.

DOO-DADS. You shoulda figgered this one out by yourself by now.

EWE (pronounced *you*) Female sheep; Do you know how to make a u-turn? Grab her by the ears.

HEIFER. Young female cow.

FILLY. Young female cowhorse.

FILLYOSSIFY. Wise words (more or less) spoken by a life worn old cowboy (**fillyossifer**).

COLT. (1) young horse; (2) Brand of shootin' iron.

WORKHORSE. Much bigger than a cowhorse; A very powerful horse with great big hooves (Feet); Two horsepower of workhorses could pull a 60 horsepower pickup out of the mud or a snowbank; Whoever figured out automobile horsepower never worked with a real workhorse.

PLUG. (1) Wad of tobacco stuffed inside the mouth for chawin' on—makin' the cowboy look like a squirrel with a mouthful of nuts; (2) Horse too old and tired to ever buck. Also called a **nag**, or an **old nag**.

Gross rated section:

BRAND. A legally registered trademark burned into the hide of a critter to indicate ownership, not enjoyed by the critter near as much as by the cowboy; You all know one brand, the—B Q. Do you get it yet? The Bar B Q. Still don't get it? Oh, come on! it's the Barbeque.

BRANDING. The process of burning the mark into the hide of the critter; Also refers to the entire process—branding, earmarking, castrating, vaccinating, etc.

BRANDING IRON. Tool heated up in a fire and used to burn a brand into the hide of a critter.

EARMARK. Another indication of ownership; With a very sharp kinfe, remove pieces of the cowcritter's ear to give it a distinctive shape; Process very much disliked by the cowcritter.

DEWLAP. Another indication of ownership; With a very sharp knife, cut loose a piece of skin under the throat of the cowcritter, left attached at one end so that the piece of skin dangles, easily visible for the owner to identify his critter; A process very much disliked by the cowcritter.

WATTLE. Same as a **dewlap** except at some other location on the cowcritter.

MARK (MARKING). The process of whacking loose parts of the cowcritter for making his ownership visibly recognizable.

CUT (Castrate). Using a very sharp knife, remove the **doo-dads** from the male critter rendering him unable to breed. The critter very, very, VERY much did *not* like this process.

DOCK (DOCKING). With a very sharp knife remove the tail of a lamb—a very disliked process for the lamb. The ewe lambs tails are cut real short, for breeding accessibility. The male lambs tails are left a little longer. It is a health hazard for sheep to have their naturally long tails, as feces and other junk tends to cling to the wooly tails. Every **Basko** should know this.

BLM. (Bureau of Land Management) Bureaucracy that regulates certain federal lands on which a rancher might be permitted to run some of his cattle; Often deemed to be the enemy; A bunch of gung ho college graduates who never had any dirt under their fingernails, or **cow stuff** on their boots, who have power to put a rancher out of business by the stroke of a pen on some federal regulation.

WINDMILL. Very important wind driven machine for lifting water out of the hole in the ground, called a **well**; A **well** was made by digging a hole in the ground with a pick and shovel.

BOB-WIRE. (Barbed wire) Wire with sharp metal points attached, used for making fences to keep cows in a field; Designed specifically for cutting a man to shreds; Sometimes did the same to cattle and horses.

BOB-WIRE FENCE. (1) Item which fell over allowing cows to go to the other side; A horse would go to the other side too; However if the horse was carrying a rider, then there was almost nothing in the world could make that horse cross to the other side of a fallen bob-wire fence; (2) Birth control device placed between cows and bulls to keep them from getting together and breeding at the wrong season; Didn't always work.

CRAZY AS A BEDBUG. Crazy but harmless.

MAD AS A WET HEN. Mad.

MAD ENOUGH TO CHEW HORSESHOES AND SPIT OUT NAILS. Madder than a wet hen.

MEANER THAN A ROCKPILE FULL OF RATTLESNAKES. Really mean.

HUNGRY ENOUGH TO EAT THE NORTH END OF A SOUTHBOUND SKUNK. Very hungry; Very, very hungry.

ENOUGH TO GAG A MAGGOT OFF A GUT WAGON. Very bad smell.

CHURCH. Non-existent item on the Madeline Plains.

BAR. Existent item.

GAY. Word used in old time cowboy and country songs, meaning happy; Never used for what it means today; There was another word for that, but I ain't gonna tell it to you.

BREAKFAST. Only way to start a day—with a hearty one.

DINNER. Very hearty main meal of the day, served at noon.

SUPPER. Evening meal; Light evening meal.

LUNCH. Noon meal at school; Meal in a sack for when the cowboy was away from the ranch house at mid-day.